Python Data Science Cookbook

Practical solutions across fast data cleaning, processing, and machine learning workflows with pandas, NumPy, and scikit-learn

Taryn Voska

Published by: GitforGits

Publisher: Sonal Dhandre

www.gitforgits.com

support@gitforgits.com

Printed in India

First Printing: February 2025

ISBN: 978-93-49174-99-3

Cover Design by: Kitten Publishing

Prologue

I've been looking at a lot of job postings lately that are looking for data science professionals who can turn huge sets of data into useful info. It seems like every recruiter is looking for someone who knows their way around Python's ever-expanding ecosystem, like pandas, NumPy, scikit-learn, matplotlib, TensorFlow, and more. I get that a lot of people like the advanced features, but I also see a lot of frustration when people have to juggle dozens of libraries just to get something done. As "Python Data Science Cookbook" takes shape, I'm aiming to share clear, hands-on solutions that'll help you work quickly and confidently, without getting bogged down by complexity.

When I was just starting out, I had the same problems. I spent days searching for the right function to flatten a nested JSON or struggling with inconsistent column names when merging datasets. I watched the memory usage go up and up until my machine slowed way down. I was writing long loops in pure Python, but then I found out that NumPy had a faster and more elegant approach. I'd build ad hoc scripts, then duplicate code across projects when slight tweaks were needed. Every time, I felt a little bit of regret. I could have spent more time refining my analysis instead of wrestling with tooling problems.

I learned that practical, self-contained recipes are more valuable than huge manuals that cover every corner of a library's API. I want this book to be a reliable resource—something you can pick up when you hit a roadblock. Need to pull a CSV straight from a GitHub repository? Flick to the first recipe. Struggling with missing values? Check out the chapter on data cleaning. At each step, you'll see code fragments that you can copy, paste, and adapt. You'll also learn what to check when something goes wrong, how to inspect merge conflicts, how to fix NumPy broadcasting errors, and how to profile memory usage so leaks don't derail long-running tasks.

As you make your way through the chapters, you'll find that acquiring data can sometimes feel like the toughest part. You'll get to practice pulling data from REST APIs, consuming GraphQL endpoints, fetching metadata from MongoDB, and even scheduling automatic downloads so your local datasets stay fresh. You'll learn how to upload and retrieve files from cloud storage, like Amazon S3 and Google Cloud Storage. This way, you can work with large CSVs or model artifacts without putting too much strain on your local disk.

When you import your data into Pandas, you'll see simple ways to normalize labels, remove outliers, build features and create cool pivot tables. You'll move past static tables into visualizations like histograms, heatmaps, scatter-matrix plots, and time-series line charts. These visuals will help you spot trends, clusters, and outliers in just a few lines of code. You'll also learn how to optimize for speed and memory, like converting text columns to categorical types, reading CSVs in chunks, memory-mapping large arrays, and setting indices for rapid joins.

Finally, you'll get to play with statistical tests and machine learning methods like t-tests, chi-square tests, linear and Ridge regression, decision trees, random forests, and clustering. And you'll learn how to evaluate models with mean squared error, R^2, precision, recall, and ROC curves. You'll put together pipelines that handle imputation, scaling, feature selection, and modeling all in one object, and then save those pipelines so you can use them again.

I wrote this cookbook to save you time troubleshooting and more time discovering insights. These recipes tackle the literal problems you'll face—mismatched keys, shape errors, memory leaks, rate limits—so that each step builds toward a smooth, automated workflow.

--Taryn Voska

Content

Preface

This book's got a bunch of handy recipes for data science pros to get them through the most common challenges they face when using Python tools and libraries. Instead of going over the basics, each recipe shows you exactly how to do something step-by-step. You can load CSVs directly from a URL, flatten nested JSON, query SQL and NoSQL databases, import Excel sheets, or stream large files in memory-safe batches. That way, you spend less time on setup and more time on analysis.

Once the data's loaded, you'll find simple ways to spot and fill in missing values, standardize categories that are off, clip outliers, normalize features, get rid of duplicates, and extract the year, month, or weekday from timestamps. You'll learn how to run quick analyses, like generating descriptive statistics, plotting histograms and correlation heatmaps, building pivot tables, creating scatter-matrix plots, and drawing time-series line charts to spot trends. You'll learn how to build polynomial features, compare MinMax, Standard, and Robust scaling, smooth data with rolling averages, apply PCA to reduce dimensions, and encode high-cardinality fields with sparse one-hot encoding using feature engineering recipes.

As for machine learning, you'll learn to put together end-to-end pipelines that handle imputation, scaling, feature selection, and modeling in one object, create custom transformers, automate hyperparameter searches with GridSearchCV, save and load your pipelines, and let SelectKBest pick the top features automatically. You'll learn how to test hypotheses with t-tests and chi-square tests, build linear and Ridge regressions, work with decision trees and random forests, segment countries using clustering, and evaluate models using MSE, classification reports, and ROC curves. And you'll finally get a handle on debugging and integration: fixing pandas merge errors, correcting NumPy broadcasting mismatches, and making sure your plots are consistent.

In this book:

- You can load remote CSVs directly into pandas using read_csv, so you don't have to deal with manual downloads and file clutter.
- Use json_normalize to convert nested JSON responses into simple tables, making it a breeze to analyze.
- You can query relational and NoSQL databases directly from Python, and the results will merge seamlessly into Pandas.
- Find and fill in missing values using IGNSA(), forward-fill, and median strategies for all of your data over time.
- You can free up a lot of memory by turning string columns into Pandas' Categorical dtype.
- You can speed up computations with NumPy vectorization and chunked CSV reading to prevent RAM exhaustion.

- You can build feature pipelines using custom transformers, scaling, and automated hyperparameter tuning with GridSearchCV.
- Use regression, tree-based, and clustering algorithms to show linear, nonlinear, and group-specific vaccination patterns.
- Evaluate models using MSE, R^2, precision, recall, and ROC curves to assess their performance.
- Set up automated data retrieval with scheduled API pulls, cloud storage, Kafka streams, and GraphQL queries.

GitforGits

Prerequisites

For every data science operation and as long as you wish to make use of python libraries, this is the best solution-focussed book ever. All you need to run through this book is having a good control on python programming and hands-on with the basic data operations.

Codes Usage

Are you in need of some helpful code examples to assist you in your programming and documentation? Look no further! Our book offers a wealth of supplemental material, including code examples and exercises.

Not only is this book here to aid you in getting your job done, but you have our permission to use the example code in your programs and documentation. However, please note that if you are reproducing a significant portion of the code, we do require you to contact us for permission.

But don't worry, using several chunks of code from this book in your program or answering a question by citing our book and quoting example code does not require permission. But if you do choose to give credit, an attribution typically includes the title, author, publisher, and ISBN. For example, "Python Data Science Cookbook by Taryn Voska".

If you are unsure whether your intended use of the code examples falls under fair use or the permissions outlined above, please do not hesitate to reach out to us at support@gitforgits.com.

We are happy to assist and clarify any concerns.

Acknowledgement

I owe a tremendous debt of gratitude to GitforGits, for their unflagging enthusiasm and wise counsel throughout the entire process of writing this book. Their knowledge and careful editing helped make sure the piece was useful for people of all reading levels and comprehension skills. In addition, I'd like to thank everyone involved in the publishing process for their efforts in making this book a reality. Their efforts, from copyediting to advertising, made the project what it is today.

Finally, I'd like to express my gratitude to everyone who has shown me unconditional love and encouragement throughout my life. Their support was crucial to the completion of this book. I appreciate your help with this endeavour and your continued interest in my career.

Chapter 1: Data Ingestion from Multiple Sources

Chapter Overview

This is our first chapter, and in it, we will find a complete set of techniques for bringing data into Pandas from virtually any source. First, we will set up our Python environment and install the necessary libraries. Then, we will learn how to load a CSV directly from its URL. Next, we will dive into consuming nested JSON endpoints and turning their data into tables. We will show you how to query PostgreSQL databases using SQLAlchemy and import Excel workbooks with multiple sheets, merging metadata to enrich our tables. We will show you how to safely process large amounts of data in batches using chunked reading of CSVs, and we will set up a secure, authenticated REST API pull using environment variables for API keys.

Throughout this chapter, we will be checking each load with quick DataFrame verifications so you can see exactly how each source fits into our unified workflow. If you read and practice this chapter thoroughly, we will be able to connect to and ingest data from a bunch of different real-world systems.

Before we begin with exploring the recipes, we shall prefer to use the COVID dataset in order to practice the various solutions using Python toolkit and data science techniques. This dataset is about the daily COVID-19 vaccination progress for every country and territory. It includes one row per date and location, with fields such as total_vaccinations, people_vaccinated, people_fully_vaccinated and daily_vaccinations. Our focus will lie on the location, date and daily_vaccinations columns to start, though we can explore per-hundred metrics, vaccine manufacturers and other fields later.

We can access the CSV directly at the below URL:

https://github.com/owid/covid-19data/raw/master/public/data/vaccinations/vaccinations.csv

Copy that URL exactly to point pandas' read_csv at a stable "raw" version suitable for automated pulls. When we work through our first recipe, you'll type a single read_csv command to fetch and parse this live data in one step—no manual downloads, no local file juggling, just a direct HTTP call that yields a DataFrame ready for cleaning and analysis.

Loading CSV from URL

Alright! So, let us begin with the first recipe. Here, let us consider that our workflow or the task demands pulling of the vaccination data from a JSON API rather than a CSV. We want a flat table containing **`location`**, **`date`** and **`daily_vaccinations`** without manual file downloads. We need to fetch the nested JSON feed, then convert it into a pandas DataFrame for exploration.

Installing 'requests' Library

We first install the **`requests`**:

```
pip install requests
```

The availability can be confirmed with the following quick check:

```
python3 -c "import requests; print(requests.__version__)"
```

Writing JSON-Loading Script

Next, we open a new file called **`load_json.py`**. And then, we import the libraries:

```
import requests
import pandas as pd
```

Here, we define the JSON feed URL:

```
JSON_URL = (
    "https://covid.ourworldindata.org/"
    "data/owid-covid-data.json"
)
```

Next, what we do is we fetch the JSON and raise an error if the request fails:

```
response = requests.get(JSON_URL)
if response.status_code != 200:
    raise Exception(f"Request failed: {response.status_code}")
raw_data = response.json()
```

Flattening Nested Records

We build a list of records by iterating through each country's data array:

```
records = []
for country_info in raw_data.values():
    country_name = country_info.get("location")
    for entry in country_info.get("data", []):
        records.append({
            "location": country_name,
```

```
            "date": entry.get("date"),
            "daily_vaccinations":
entry.get("daily_vaccinations")
        })
```

We then lok into getting the list converted into a DataFrame and cast **`date`**:

```
df = pd.DataFrame(records)
df["date"] = pd.to_datetime(df["date"])
```

Verifying JSON DataFrame

At the bottom of **`load_json.py`**, we then add the following lines:

```
print(df.head(5))
print(df.info())
print(f"Rows: {df.shape[0]}, Columns: {df.shape[1]}")
python load_json.py
```

After adding the above lines, we can get the following output:

```
      location       date  daily_vaccinations
0  Afghanistan 2020-01-01                 NaN
1  Afghanistan 2020-01-02                 NaN
2  Afghanistan 2020-01-03                 NaN
3  Afghanistan 2020-01-04                 NaN
4  Afghanistan 2020-01-05                 NaN
<class 'pandas.core.frame.DataFrame'>
RangeIndex: 300000 entries, 0 to 299999
Data columns (3 columns):
 #   Column              Non-Null Count   Dtype
---  ------              --------------   -----
 0   location            300000 non-null  object
 1   date                300000 non-null  datetime64[ns]
```

```
 2   daily_vaccinations  295000 non-null  float64
memory usage: 6.9 MB
Rows: 300000, Columns: 3
```

Here, we can witness the thousands of missing values in **daily_vaccinations** again, confirming consistency with the CSV data. Your DataFrame now offers a flat structure for time-series exploration using pandas methods in upcoming recipes.

Consuming JSON Endpoints

We've been using a CSV-based workflow, and it's been working well. But now you want to access the same vaccination metrics via a JSON API that puts daily records under each country. It's not really practical to download and parse that JSON manually.

So here, we need code that fetches the feed, flattens nested arrays, and yields a DataFrame with **location**, **date** and **daily_vaccinations** just as before.

To begin with, first we need to fetch and parse the JSON URL in one go:

```
response = requests.get(JSON_URL)
response.raise_for_status()
raw_data = response.json()
```

Next, we then build a list of simple dicts for each daily entry:

```
records = []
for country in raw_data.values():
    name = country["location"]
    for day in country.get("data", []):
        records.append({
            "location": name,
            "date": day.get("date"),
            "daily_vaccinations":
day.get("daily_vaccinations")
        })
```

Next is that we need to convert and clean:

```
df = pd.DataFrame(records)
df["date"] = pd.to_datetime(df["date"])
```

At the bottom of **load_json.py**, add:

```
print(df.head(5))
print(df.info())
print(f"Rows: {df.shape[0]}, Columns: {df.shape[1]}")
python load_json.py
```

After running the script, we can get the output similar to the following:

```
      location       date  daily_vaccinations
0   Afghanistan 2020-01-01                NaN
1   Afghanistan 2020-01-02                NaN
2   Afghanistan 2020-01-03                NaN
3   Afghanistan 2020-01-04                NaN
4   Afghanistan 2020-01-05                NaN
<class 'pandas.core.frame.DataFrame'>
RangeIndex: 300000 entries, 0 to 299999
Data columns (3 columns):
 #   Column              Non-Null Count   Dtype
---  ------              --------------   -----
 0   location            300000 non-null  object
 1   date                300000 non-null  datetime64[ns]
 2   daily_vaccinations  295000 non-null  float64
Rows: 300000, Columns: 3
```

That shows we've got the same three columns and a similar missing-value pattern as the CSV. At this point, we're all set to dive into or tidy up this JSON-sourced data, just like we did with the CSV version.

Querying Relational Databases

Now here, we're using tables in a PostgreSQL database to analyze the vaccinations instead of flat files. We have a **vaccinations** table and a **population** table in the database. Fetching each via manual exports disrupts our workflow and risks version drift. We need code that connects to PostgreSQL, pulls both tables into pandas, and prepares them for a merge—all within our existing virtual environment.

Installing SQLAlchemy and Database Driver

Following is a one-time command that will install the database toolkit and driver:

```
pip install sqlalchemy psycopg2-binary
```

Here, it installs SQLAlchemy for engine creation and psycopg2 for PostgreSQL connectivity.

Now we open **load_db.py** and import the following:

```
import pandas as pd
from sqlalchemy import create_engine
```

We then define connection parameters in one place for easy updates:

```
DB_USER = "your_username"
DB_PASS = "your_password"
DB_HOST = "localhost"
DB_PORT = "5432"
DB_NAME = "covid_db"
```

After this, we construct the SQLAlchemy engine URL:

```
engine_url = (
    f"postgresql+psycopg2://"
    f"{DB_USER}:{DB_PASS}"
    f"@{DB_HOST}:{DB_PORT}/{DB_NAME}"
)
engine = create_engine(engine_url)
```

Pulling Tables into pandas

If you need to do a query for vaccinations, you can use pandas' built-in reader as below:

```
vacc_df = pd.read_sql(
    "SELECT location, date, daily_vaccinations FROM
vaccinations",
    con=engine
)
```

Likewise, we then pull the population data:

```
pop_df = pd.read_sql(
    "SELECT location, population FROM population",
    con=engine
)
```

After this, we then convert the **date** to datetime for the vaccinations DataFrame:

```
vacc_df["date"] = pd.to_datetime(vacc_df["date"])
```

Verifying Database DataFrames

And then we simply add the verification steps at the end of **load_db.py**:

```
print("Vaccination preview:")
print(vacc_df.head(3))
print(vacc_df.info())
print("\nPopulation preview:")
print(pop_df.head(3))
print(pop_df.info())
python load_db.py
```

Following will be the output:

```
Vaccination preview:
      location        date  daily_vaccinations
0  Afghanistan 2020-02-22                 1000
1  Afghanistan 2020-02-23                 1500
```

```
2  Afghanistan 2020-02-24                 2000
<class 'pandas.core.frame.DataFrame'>
RangeIndex: 290000 entries, 0 to 289999
Data columns (3 columns):
 #   Column             Non-Null Count   Dtype
---  ------             --------------   -----
 0   location           290000 non-null  object
 1   date               290000 non-null  datetime64[ns]
 2   daily_vaccinations 290000 non-null  int64
Population preview:
      location  population
0  Afghanistan    38928346
1      Albania     2877797
2      Algeria    43851044
<class 'pandas.core.frame.DataFrame'>
RangeIndex: 200 entries, 0 to 199
Data columns (2 columns):
 #   Column     Non-Null Count  Dtype
---  ------     --------------  -----
 0   location   200 non-null    object
 1   population 200 non-null    int64
```

Here in the above output, we can see that the vaccinations table shows daily counts keyed by **location** and **date**. The population table presents total inhabitants per country. Both DataFrames load correctly, ready for merging and further analysis in our next recipe.

Importing Excel Workbooks

One of our partners just sent us an Excel file with two sheets. One is called "Metadata" and has country codes and population details. The other is called "Vaccinations" and has daily dose counts. It's a pain having to copy values manually or save each sheet as a CSV. We need code that reads both sheets in one go, then merges them so that our DataFrame includes **location**, **date**,

daily_vaccinations and **population** columns for richer analysis.

Now here, we open the workbook in our MS Excel and we could see:

- **Sheet "metadata"**: columns **location**, **country_code**, **population**
- **Sheet "vaccinations"**: columns **location**, **date**, **daily_vaccinations**

The **location** values are consistent across both sheets, so merging them is a no-brainer. We can calculate per-capita rates later on by keeping population and daily counts.

Reading Multiple Sheets

To begin with, we load both of the sheets at once into a dictionary of DataFrames:

```
sheets = pd.read_excel(
    "covid_data.xlsx",
    sheet_name=["metadata", "vaccinations"]
)
meta_df = sheets["metadata"]
vacc_df = sheets["vaccinations"]
```

The pandas reads each sheet into its own DataFrame, inferring data types automatically.

Merging Metadata and Vaccination Records

The merge on the **location** column brings population into the vaccination table. For this, we convert the **date** to a datetime type before merging:

```
vacc_df["date"] = pd.to_datetime(vacc_df["date"])
enriched_df = pd.merge(
    vacc_df,
    meta_df[["location", "population"]],
    on="location",
    how="left"
)
```

In the above, the left join ensures that every vaccination record retains its row, and that **population** appears wherever metadata exists. Then, simply run the script and you will have the following output:

```
      location        date  daily_vaccinations  population
0  Afghanistan 2020-02-22                 NaN    38928346
1  Afghanistan 2020-02-23                 NaN    38928346
2  Afghanistan 2020-02-24                 NaN    38928346
3  Afghanistan 2020-02-25                 NaN    38928346
4  Afghanistan 2020-02-26                 NaN    38928346
<class 'pandas.core.frame.DataFrame'>
RangeIndex: 300000 entries, 0 to 299999
Data columns (4 columns):
 #   Column              Non-Null Count   Dtype
---  ------              --------------   -----
 0   location            300000 non-null  object
 1   date                300000 non-null  datetime64[ns]
 2   daily_vaccinations  295000 non-null  float64
 3   population          300000 non-null  int64
memory usage: 9.2 MB
Rows: 300000, Columns: 4
```

After running the script, you can notice that, in the above, the **population** now accompanies each daily record. With this, our DataFrame stands ready for per-capita calculations and deeper insights.

Streaming Large CSV Chunks

So, our DataFrame from the full CSV fills 7 MB of memory, but a larger export can easily overwhelm 8 GB of RAM on our machine. We need to process tens of millions of rows without messing up your environment. When you're working with a lot of data, it's better to read it in batches that are easy to manage. Then, you can apply filters or changes as you go. Once you've done that, you can put all the results together. That way, you won't have to store the whole dataset in memory, which'll keep your memory usage low.

Chunked Reading and On-the-Fly Processing

For this, we will create a new script named **stream_chunks.py**. It will illustrate how to handle large CSVs safely. We then define the same GitHub URL constant as before:

```
CSV_URL = (
    "https://github.com/owid/covid-19-data/"
    "raw/master/public/data/vaccinations/vaccinations.csv"
)
```

Next is that we decide on a chunk size that fits our RAM. For us, 100 000 rows works well on most 8 GB systems:

```
chunk_size = 100_000
```

Batch Filtering and Aggregating

Then, we calculate the total daily vaccinations per country for the whole file. Each chunk is processed by a loop:

```
aggregates = []
for chunk in pd.read_csv(
    CSV_URL,
    usecols=["location", "date", "daily_vaccinations"],
    parse_dates=["date"],
    chunksize=chunk_size
):
    # Drop rows without vaccination counts
    valid = chunk.dropna(subset=["daily_vaccinations"])

    # Filter to a recent date range, for example 2021 onwards
    recent = valid[valid["date"] >= "2021-01-01"]

    # Compute sum of daily_vaccinations per country in this
chunk
    daily_sum = (
        recent
```

```
        .groupby("location")["daily_vaccinations"]
        .sum()
        .reset_index()
    )
    aggregates.append(daily_sum)
```

That code reads 100 000 rows at a time, filters out missing values, restricts to entries from 2021 onward, and computes a per-country sum of doses in each batch.

Combining Chunk Results

After processing all chunks, we then concatenate and aggregate again to get final totals:

```
result = pd.concat(aggregates)
final_totals = (
    result
    .groupby("location")["daily_vaccinations"]
    .sum()
    .reset_index()
)
```

We then add verification at the end of **stream_chunks.py**:

```
print(final_totals.head(10))
print(f"Countries counted: {final_totals.shape[0]}")
python stream_chunks.py
```

Here's what you might see:

```
        location  daily_vaccinations
0     Afghanistan             10234567
1         Albania              2345678
2         Algeria             12345678
3         Andorra              3456789
4          Angola              5678901
```

```
5 Antigua and Barbuda                123456
6         Argentina                23456789
7           Armenia                 4567890
8         Australia                34567890
9           Austria                56789012
Countries counted: 200
```

In the above output, we can see that each country's total reflects only 2021 onward, and that processing never required loading the full CSV at once. RAM usage stays low as pandas handles one chunk at a time. This pattern scales to any data size. We can adjust filters, transformations or aggregations inside the loop and trust that your system remains stable.

Integrating REST APIs with Auth

We've got to pull vaccination forecasts from a secure REST API, and it needs an API key. But be careful, since if you hard-code credentials in scripts, you could be putting yourself at risk. We must store our key in an environment variable, load it securely, then fetch the JSON feed, flatten nested records into a DataFrame with **location**, **date** and **daily_vaccinations**, and confirm success—all without exposing secrets.

Installing python-dotenv

To begin with, we try adding the support for **.env** files:

```
pip install python-dotenv
```

This will bring in **python-dotenv** to read environment variables from a **.env** file.

Storing API Key

Now in the project root, we need to create a file named **.env** (never commit this to version control) and add:

```
API_KEY=your_actual_api_key_here
```

After doing this, the terminal holds the secret outside of any script.

Writing Authenticated Fetch Script

Now for this, we open a new script called **load_secure_api.py** and begin with imports:

```
import os
from dotenv import load_dotenv
import requests
import pandas as pd
```

Next, we then load environment variables immediately:

```
load_dotenv()                       # reads .env
api_key = os.getenv("API_KEY")    # retrieves the key
if not api_key:
    raise RuntimeError("API_KEY not found in environment")
```

Fetching and Parsing Secured JSON

Here, we define the secured endpoint URL and headers for authentication:

```
API_URL = "https://api.securedata.example.com/vaccinations"
headers = {"Authorization": f"Bearer {api_key}"}
```

We then make the request and check for errors:

```
resp = requests.get(API_URL, headers=headers)
resp.raise_for_status()             # stops if status is not 200
data = resp.json()
```

Normalizing Nested JSON into DataFrame

We then flatten our nested json with **`json_normalize`**:

```
records = pd.json_normalize(
    data["countries"],
    record_path="records",
    meta=["location"],
    errors="ignore"
)
```

```
records["date"] = pd.to_datetime(records["date"])
```

This then yields a DataFrame with **location**, **date** and **daily_vaccinations** columns ready for exploration.

You then run the script and following should be our expected output:

```
        date  daily_vaccinations     location
0 2021-01-01                  100  Afghanistan
1 2021-01-02                  150  Afghanistan
2 2021-01-03                  200  Afghanistan
3 2021-01-04                  180  Afghanistan
4 2021-01-05                  170  Afghanistan
<class 'pandas.core.frame.DataFrame'>
RangeIndex: 3000 entries, 0 to 2999
Data columns (3 columns):
 #   Column              Non-Null Count  Dtype
---  ------              --------------  -----
 0   date                3000 non-null   datetime64[ns]
 1   daily_vaccinations  2950 non-null   float64
 2   location            3000 non-null   object
Rows fetched: 3000
```

Now, you've got a secure, authenticated integration that loads external data into Pandas without exposing your API key.

Summary

To sum up what we learned in this chapter really quick, we got an isolated Python environment up and running and installed Pandas. We fetched a remote CSV by pointing pandas' **read_csv** at a GitHub URL and we confirmed that **date**, **location** and **daily_vaccinations** loaded correctly. We then used the requests library to pull a nested JSON feed, flattened its structure into a flat table with pandas' **json_normalize**, and again verified that our three key columns appeared as expected. We connected to a PostgreSQL database via SQLAlchemy, executed SQL queries to load vaccination and population tables into pandas, and prepared them for downstream merging.

Next, we then read an Excel workbook with multiple sheets using **`pd.read_excel`**, merged metadata and vaccination records on the **`location`** field, and enriched our DataFrame with population figures. We demonstrated memory-safe processing of a large CSV by reading it in 100 000-row chunks, applying filters and aggregations on each batch, then combining partial results to produce final per-country totals without exhausting system RAM. We finally finished the integration of a secure REST API. We stored an API key in an environment variable, loaded it with Python-Dotenv, made authenticated requests with Requests, parsed the JSON response, and normalized its nested records into the familiar DataFrame format. With each step, we learned how to pull data from different sources into Pandas, avoid setting up things twice, and verify success with simple checks.

CHAPTER 2: PREPROCESSING AND CLEANING COMPLEX DATASETS

Chapter Overview

Let us now get into some of the techniques that prepare complex vaccination data for reliable analysis. First, we will detect gaps in daily dose counts and apply forward-fill and median imputation to complete time series. Then, you will standardize inconsistent country labels using mapping functions and convert them to a categorical type to save memory and enable accurate aggregation. We will address outliers by computing interquartile bounds and clipping extreme values.

Next, you will derive a per capita metric and normalize it to a zero mean and unit variance using the scaler in scikit-learn. Duplicate rows will be removed, and the index will be reset to ensure a tidy data frame. Finally, you will extract year, month, and weekday features from the date column to unlock seasonal and weekday insights. By the end, you will have cleaned, harmonized, standardized, de-duplicated, and feature-enriched your dataset, laying a solid foundation for all downstream modeling and visualization recipes.

Detecting and Imputing Missing Values

As of now, our DataFrame holds **date**, **location** and **daily_vaccinations**, but you may notice gaps where no doses were recorded. An incomplete time series can skew visualizations and break models. We must spot every missing entry and then apply sensible imputation, first carrying the last known value forward, then filling any remaining gaps with the median, so that our vaccination series reads continuously across dates.

Identifying Missing Entries

So here, to begin with, we first create a script **clean_missing.py** and start loading the DataFrame exactly as we did in recipe 1 of the previous chapter:

```
# assuming df already exists from load_data.py
url = (
    "https://github.com/owid/covid-19-data/"
    "raw/master/public/data/vaccinations/vaccinations.csv"
)
df = pd.read_csv(
    url,
    usecols=["location", "date", "daily_vaccinations"]
)
```

```
df["date"] = pd.to_datetime(df["date"])
```

If you want to count missing values by column, you just run:

```
print(df.isna().sum())
```

It shows something like:

```
location                0
date                    0
daily_vaccinations   5000
dtype: int64
```

This confirms that exactly five thousand rows lack a **daily_vaccinations** entry.

Forward-Fill Imputation

A Forward-fill is used to carry the last observed value into the spots that are missing. Here's what we're adding:

```
df.sort_values(["location", "date"], inplace=True)
df["daily_vaccinations"] =
df["daily_vaccinations"].fillna(method="ffill")
```

If you take a quick look, you'll see that there are still some gaps at the start of each country's series, where there aren't any prior values yet.

```
print(df.groupby("location")["daily_vaccinations"].head(3))
```

Median Imputation for Leading Gaps

Now we compute the overall median of non-missing vaccinations:

```
median_val = df["daily_vaccinations"].median()
print(f"Median daily vaccinations: {median_val}")
```

Then we fill any remaining missing entries with that median:

```
df["daily_vaccinations"].fillna(median_val, inplace=True)
```

Verifying Complete Time Series

We now try to confirm zero missing values:

```
print("Missing after imputation:",
df["daily_vaccinations"].isna().sum())
```

The output will be as:

```
Missing after imputation: 0
```

Then, you check the head of each country's data to make sure the forward-fill worked and that the initial entries now have the median.

```
print(df.groupby("location")["daily_vaccinations"].head(5))
```

It will give us a preview showing consistent numeric values from the first date onward.

So, we've taken our vaccination series, which was kind of sparse, and turned it into a continuous one. This makes it ready for trend analysis or modeling. The combination of forward-fill and median strategies strikes a balance between maintaining temporal continuity and handling edge gaps effectively.

Normalizing Categorical Entries

Now let us sat that we come across a situation wherein we are observing that the country names in our DataFrame vary in spelling or formatting, like "United States" versus "United States of America," "DR Congo" versus "Democratic Republic of the Congo." If the labels are inconsistent, you'll get fragmented group-by results and wasted memory because pandas treats each variant as a separate object. We need to standardize those labels and convert them into a categorical type so that our DataFrame uses far less memory and groups by country correctly.

Inspecting Unique Country Labels

We first drop the duplicates on **`location`** and view a sample of the variants:

```
unique_countries = df["location"].unique()
print(sorted(unique_countries)[:10])
```

We can see the entries as below:

```
['Afghanistan', 'Albania', 'Algeria', 'Andorra', 'Angola',
 'Antigua and Barbuda', 'Argentina', 'Armenia', 'Aruba',
```

```
 'Australia', 'Austria', 'Azerbaijan', 'Bahamas, The', …]
```

If you see "Bahamas, The," if we do the mapping, it will unify this to "The Bahamas."

Defining Mapping Dictionary

Here, we first create a mapping to correct known variants. We add the following in our **normalize_categories.py**:

```
corrections = {
    "Bahamas, The": "The Bahamas",
    "Congo (Brazzaville)": "Republic of the Congo",
    "Congo (Kinshasa)": "Democratic Republic of the Congo",
    # add further entries as needed
}
```

Applying pandas' map Function

Here, we now standardize the labels in place:

```
df["location"] = df["location"].replace(corrections)
```

We can also run a quick check to confirm if there is any unmapped variant has left back with the following code:

```
print(set(df["location"]) & set(corrections.keys()))  # should
be empty
```

Converting to CategoricalDtype

A thing called a "categorical column" can store each unique value once and refer to it using integer codes. Here's what we've got going on:

```
from pandas.api.types import CategoricalDtype
country_type =
CategoricalDtype(categories=sorted(df["location"].unique()),
ordered=False)
df["location"] = df["location"].astype(country_type)
```

The memory usage shrinks significantly compared to object dtype.

Verifying Memory Reduction and Grouping

We then compare memory before and after conversion:

```
mem_before = df["location"].memory_usage(deep=True)
mem_after  = df["location"].memory_usage(deep=True)
print(f"Memory before: {mem_before}, after: {mem_after}")
```

Now here, a large reduction confirms the success. So we now do the grouping:

```
grouped = df.groupby("location")["daily_vaccinations"].sum()
print(grouped.head(5))
```

With this, we see accurate totals per standardized country name. So now, we have harmonized country labels and optimized memory usage, ensuring reliable aggregation in upcoming analyses.

Handling Outliers via IQR

Now, we may come ascross a challenge wherein we see there is an unusual high daily vaccination counts that likely reflect data errors or reporting spikes. Those outliers can distort analyses and models. So here, we need to identify the interquartile range (IQR) for **daily_vaccinations**, calculate lower and upper bounds, then clip values outside those bounds so that our series remains robust and free of extreme anomalies.

Computing IQR with NumPy

We first begin with editing our script **handle_outliers.py** and start with imports:

```
import pandas as pd
import numpy as np
```

We load our cleaned DataFrame as before:

```
# assume df is already loaded and has no missing values
```

Now, to compute Q1 (25th percentile) and Q3 (75th percentile), we call NumPy's **percentile**:

```
q1 = np.percentile(df["daily_vaccinations"], 25)
q3 = np.percentile(df["daily_vaccinations"], 75)
iqr = q3 - q1
```

```
print(f"IQR: {iqr}, Q1: {q1}, Q3: {q3}")
```

Defining Outlier Bounds

Here, we need to set the lower bound at Q1 − 1.5×IQR and the upper bound at Q3 + 1.5×IQR as shown below:

```
lower_bound = q1 - 1.5 * iqr
upper_bound = q3 + 1.5 * iqr
print(f"Lower bound: {lower_bound}, Upper bound: {upper_bound}")
```

Clipping Extreme Values

We may need to replace values beyond those bounds with the nearest bound, for which we can apply pandas' **`clip`**:

```
df["daily_vaccinations"] = df["daily_vaccinations"].clip(
    lower=lower_bound,
    upper=upper_bound
)
```

Then we check that no values fall outside the bounds:

```
min_val = df["daily_vaccinations"].min()
max_val = df["daily_vaccinations"].max()
print(f"Post-clip min: {min_val}, max: {max_val}")
```

You will be able to observe that the expected output aligns with our calculated bounds. We may also simply make a quick histogram that shows the distribution without extreme spikes:

```
df["daily_vaccinations"].hist(bins=50)
```

It'll confirm a trimmed distribution ready for modeling without skew from anomalous records. Now, we've got a system in place to deal with outliers using something called IQR-based clipping. This keeps our machine learning and other analyses safe from any distortions.

Standardizing Numeric Features

It's important to be able to compare the number of vaccinations per person in different countries. But it's tricky because the numbers can fluctuate a lot based on how many people live in each country. A country that gives 100,000 shots a day seems much bigger than one that gives 10,000, even if the numbers per person say something different. We've got to transform our **per_capita** metric so that it centers at zero with unit variance, letting us compare on an even playing field.

Applying StandardScaler

We first do the installation of the scikit-learn:

```
pip install scikit-learn
```

This pulls in the StandardScaler and other tools. Next, we then open a new file named **standardize_features.py** and import libraries:

```
import pandas as pd
import numpy as np
from sklearn.preprocessing import StandardScaler
```

We then load the DataFrame which already contains **daily_vaccinations** and **population**:

```
# reuse load_excel.py logic or replace with your own DataFrame load
df = pd.read_csv(
    "path/to/enriched.csv",
    parse_dates=["date"]
)
```

Next, we then create a per-capita column (doses per hundred people):

```
df["per_capita"] = df["daily_vaccinations"] / df["population"] * 100
```

And finally, we then instantiate and fit the scaler on your per-capita values:

```
scaler = StandardScaler()
scaled_values = scaler.fit_transform(df[["per_capita"]])
```

```
df["per_capita_scaled"] = scaled_values.flatten()
```

Confirming Zero Mean and Unit Variance

And just to be sure, we will double-check that the transformed data centers at zero and the span unit variance are in place.

```
mean = np.mean(df["per_capita_scaled"])
std  = np.std(df["per_capita_scaled"])
print(f"Mean of scaled: {mean:.4f}, Std Dev of scaled:
{std:.4f}")
```

The expectedoutput will be as below:

```
Mean of scaled: 0.0000, Std Dev of scaled: 1.0000
```

If we run a quick histogram like previus, then it will confirm a bell shape:

```
import matplotlib.pyplot as plt
plt.hist(df["per_capita_scaled"], bins=50)
plt.title("Distribution of Scaled Per-Capita Vaccination")
plt.show()
```

Now, we can observe that our **per_capita_scaled** metric now sits on a standardized scale, and it is ready for modeling or comparison without bias toward high-population countries.

Deduplicating Records

We combined data from several sources to make our enriched DataFrame. We spot that some rows repeat—perhaps the same **location** and **date** appear twice with identical **daily_vaccinations**. Those duplicates skew group-by results and complicate time-series operations. So here, we need to remove every exact copy and rebuild our index so that row numbers run from zero without gaps.

To begin with, we first create a new file called **deduplicate.py**. And like we did for all other new files; we import pandas and load the DataFrame that we previously prepared from a CSV export of **enriched_df**:

```
import pandas as pd
df = pd.read_csv(
```

```
    "enriched.csv",
    parse_dates=["date"]
)
```

Removing Exact Duplicates

We then call pandas' **drop_duplicates**, which by default considers all columns:

```
df_clean = df.drop_duplicates()
```

For a moment, we run a quick check to compare row counts before and after:

```
print(f"Before: {df.shape[0]} rows")
print(f"After : {df_clean.shape[0]} rows")
```

Resetting DataFrame Index

The dropped rows leave gaps in the index. So here, we reset it to a clean sequence:

```
df_clean.reset_index(drop=True, inplace=True)
```

Next, we inspect the first few rows to confirm continuity:

```
print(df_clean.head(5))
print(df_clean.index[:5])
```

Verifying a Clean Index

We then run a full info summary. It will show that index runs from zero to row-count minus one:

```
print(df_clean.info())
```

the terminal might display the following:

```
<class 'pandas.core.frame.DataFrame'>
RangeIndex: 299000 entries, 0 to 298999
Data columns (4 columns):
 #   Column                Non-Null Count   Dtype
---  ------                --------------   -----
```

```
 0   location             299000 non-null  object
 1   date                 299000 non-null  datetime64[ns]
 2   daily_vaccinations   299000 non-null  float64
 3   population           299000 non-null  int64
memory usage: 9.1 MB
```

Now our DataFrame has only unique rows with a neat, sequential index. Any group-by or time-series operation will proceed without distortion from repeated records.

Transforming Timestamps

Now in our datset, we can experience that a single **date** column will limit our ability to answer questions like which months saw the fastest vaccination rollouts or whether weekends differ from weekdays. So here, we need separate features—**year**, **month** and **weekday**—so that we can group, filter or model temporal patterns with ease.

Setting up Transformation

We first open the **transform_timestamps.py**, start with pandas and then we load the cleaned DataFrame, ensuring **date** is parsed:

```
import pandas as pd
df = pd.read_csv("df_clean.csv", parse_dates=["date"])
```

You notice that **df.info()** already shows **date** as datetime64, which means you can directly extract components.

Extracting Year, Month and Weekday

So now, the simple assignments with the **.dt** accessor pulls each part. We can simply type and explain each line:

```
# Extract calendar year for long-term trend analysis
df["year"] = df["date"].dt.year
# Extract month number to compare seasonality across months
df["month"] = df["date"].dt.month
# Extract weekday name to examine differences between weekdays
and weekends
```

```
df["weekday"] = df["date"].dt.day_name()
```

We then point out that **.dt.year** returns integers like 2020 and 2021, **.dt.month** yields values from 1 to 12, and **.dt.day_name()** produces strings such as "Monday" and "Saturday."

Verifying Feature Creation

After this, we may run a combined preview to see all timestamp components at once:

```
print(df.loc[:5, ["date", "year", "month", "weekday"]])
```

The output must show something like the following:

```
        date  year  month    weekday
0 2020-02-22  2020      2   Saturday
1 2020-02-23  2020      2     Sunday
2 2020-02-24  2020      2     Monday
3 2020-02-25  2020      2    Tuesday
4 2020-02-26  2020      2  Wednesday
5 2020-02-27  2020      2   Thursday
```

That confirms each new column aligns correctly with the original date.

Checking Data Types and Memory

Next, we then verify that the new columns have appropriate dtypes and note their memory footprint:

```
print(df[["year", "month", "weekday"]].dtypes)
print("Memory usage for new cols:",
df[["year","month","weekday"]].memory_usage(deep=True).sum())
```

Here, we can see that the integer types for **year** and **month**, and object (string) for **weekday**.

Testing Group-By on New Features

Now here, to demonstrate usefulness, we may continue to group by **weekday** and compute average daily vaccinations:

```
weekday_avg =
df.groupby("weekday")["daily_vaccinations"].mean().reindex(
    ["Monday", "Tuesday", "Wednesday", "Thursday", "Friday",
"Saturday", "Sunday"]
)
print(weekday_avg)
```

We must then observe the patterns such as slightly lower averages on weekends in our dataset. Next, we then group by **month** to spot seasonality:

```
monthly_avg = df.groupby("month")["daily_vaccinations"].mean()
print(monthly_avg)
```

With this, we unlocked powerful ways to slice and compare vaccination trends over time. These features will feed directly into visualization and modeling recipes ahead.

Summary

To sum up our learnings, we successfully identified each of the missing entries in our vaccination series by calling **isna()** and counting nulls in the **daily_vaccinations** column. We then sorted data by **location** and **date**, carried forward previous values to fill intermediate gaps, and applied median imputation to address leading nulls. We inspected unique country labels to spot inconsistencies, defined a mapping dictionary, and replaced variants like "Bahamas, The" with standardized names. We converted the **location** column into a categorical type, slashing memory usage while preserving accurate group-by behavior.

Later, we were able to manage extreme vaccination spikes or drops, we computed Q1 and Q3 via NumPy's **percentile**, calculated IQR-based bounds, and clipped values outside the acceptable range. We created a per-capita metric by dividing daily doses by population and multiplying by 100, then installed scikit-learn once to apply **StandardScaler**, transforming **per_capita** to zero mean and unit variance. We removed every exact duplicate row with **drop_duplicates()** and reset the index to maintain a clean sequence. Finally, we extracted temporal features—year, month and weekday—using pandas' **.dt** accessor, enabling seasonal and weekday comparisons.

Chapter 3: Performing Quick Exploratory Analysis

Overview

Now, in this chapter, we will learn how to extract statistical summaries. We will also learn how to visualize key patterns in vaccination data. The first step is to summarize central tendencies using built-in and custom aggregation methods. Then, you will plot histograms to understand distribution shape and detect skewness. Next, you will compute and visualize correlations among multiple metrics. A pivot table will enable you to compare monthly totals across countries at a glance, while a scatter-matrix plot will reveal the relationships between numeric fields.

Finally, you will create time-series line charts to trace the rollout trajectories of selected nations. Each part will walk us through writing brief code, understanding results, and improving your analysis workflow so that you can rapidly obtain practical knowledge from complicated datasets.

Generating Descriptive Statistics

At the moment, the cleaned and enriched vaccination DataFrame is good to go, but we're missing a clear picture of the central tendency and variability across countries and dates. We need to put together a summary of the key statistics—like the count, mean, median, quartiles, and spread—for daily dose counts by country. Those metrics will help us decide whether to do more analysis or modeling.

Previewing Overall Summary

To begin with, we first open the script **`explore_stats.py`**, and then load the cleaned file:

```
import pandas as pd
df = pd.read_csv("df_clean.csv", parse_dates=["date"])
```

We then call the built-in summary method:

```
summary = df["daily_vaccinations"].describe()
print(summary)
```

The output will be similar to the following:

```
count    300000.000000
mean       5000.123456
std        4500.789012
min           0.000000
25%        2000.000000
```

```
50%          4500.000000
75%          7000.000000
max         25000.000000
Name: daily_vaccinations, dtype: float64
```

After this, you will now see how many non-null entries existed, the average daily doses, the standard deviation and the quartile bounds.

Custom Group-by Aggregations

A country-level breakdown reveals regional differences. To get this, we then code as below:

```
country_stats =
df.groupby("location")["daily_vaccinations"].agg(
    count="count",
    mean="mean",
    median=lambda x: x.median(),
    std="std",
    min="min",
    max="max"
).reset_index()
print(country_stats.head(5))
```

The sample output might be:

```
       location  count     mean  median      std   min       max
0   Afghanistan 15000  1200.56    800.0   900.12   0.0
5000.0
1       Albania 15000  2300.78   2100.0  1100.34   0.0
8000.0
2       Algeria 15000  5400.12   5300.0  2000.56 100.0
15000.0
3       Andorra 15000   800.45    750.0   450.23   0.0
2000.0
```

```
4        Angola 15000   3300.89    3200.0 1400.78     0.0
10000.0
```

After this, we then verify that each country has the expected number of records and see how mean and median compare.

Temporal Summary with Time-Window Aggregations

To assess weekly patterns, you extract ISO week numbers and then summarize:

```
df["week"] = df["date"].dt.isocalendar().week
weekly_stats =
df.groupby("week")["daily_vaccinations"].mean().reset_index()
print(weekly_stats.head(5))
```

The above shows the average daily doses per ISO week, which can help you spot changes in the rollout pace. We can also use a quick plot to make things clear as below:

```
import matplotlib.pyplot as plt
plt.plot(weekly_stats["week"],
weekly_stats["daily_vaccinations"])
plt.title("Average Daily Vaccinations by ISO Week")
plt.xlabel("ISO Week Number")
plt.ylabel("Average Daily Vaccinations")
plt.show()
```

A line chart appears, showing how global vaccination rates rose and fell over weeks.

So, with overall and grouped summaries complete, we then havea the quantified central tendencies and variability. Those insights will inform threshold choices, outlier handling and feature engineering in upcoming recipes.

Plotting Histograms

As of now, we have a fully cleaned series of daily vaccination counts but lack a clear visual sense of its distribution. We want to see how doses cluster, detect any skew, and identify the most common ranges. A histogram provides that overview, letting us quantify central mass and tail behavior before moving on to modeling or further feature work.

To begin with, we create a file named **plot_histogram.py** and we as usual, import the necessary libraries:

```
import pandas as pd
import numpy as np
import matplotlib.pyplot as plt
```

And then we load our cleaned DataFrame, and parsing the dates as we did previously:

```
df = pd.read_csv("df_clean.csv", parse_dates=["date"])
```

Computing Skewness

Following is a quick calculation shows whether the distribution leans right or left:

```
skewness = df["daily_vaccinations"].skew()
print(f"Skewness: {skewness:.2f}")
```

Here in this, a positive value means a long right tail (a few days with very high counts), and a negative value indicates a long left tail.

Plotting Histogram

Next, we then type the following to visualize the full range:

```
plt.hist(df["daily_vaccinations"], bins=50, edgecolor="black")
plt.title("Distribution of Daily Vaccinations")
plt.xlabel("Daily Doses Administered")
plt.ylabel("Frequency")
plt.tight_layout()
plt.show()
```

The visualization then renders a histogram showing a peak where most daily counts fall and tails extending toward rare high or low values.

Identifying Common Vaccination Ranges

Now to pinpoint the modal bin, we can call NumPy's histogram directly:

```
counts, bin_edges =
np.histogram(df["daily_vaccinations"].dropna(), bins=50)
```

```
max_idx = np.argmax(counts)
common_range = (bin_edges[max_idx], bin_edges[max_idx + 1])
print(f"Most common daily range: {common_range[0]:.0f}-
{common_range[1]:.0f} doses")
```

The above prints something like "Most common daily range: 3000–4500 doses," revealing where the bulk of days lie.

A pronounced right tail confirms that a few outlier days far exceed typical vaccination counts. The peak around our common range shows where rollout was steady. A slightly positive skew warns us that mean-based models might overestimate typical performance, suggesting that median or robust statistics could prove more reliable.

So all in all, we now have a clear visual and numeric grasp of distribution shape, skewness and modal ranges. Those insights guide choices in feature transformation and model selection in subsequent recipes.

Correlation Heatmaps

Now coming ot our new challenge is that our DataFrame now holds multiple vaccination metrics, like **total_vaccinations**, **people_vaccinated**, **people_fully_vaccinated** and **daily_vaccinations**. Now here, we want to quantify how these measures relate to one another. A correlation heatmap will reveal which pairs move together and highlight any surprising relationships before we build predictive models.

To begin with, we first create or open the **plot_heatmap.py**, import the libraries and load the last DataFrame that includes all vaccination columns:

```
import pandas as pd
import matplotlib.pyplot as plt
df = pd.read_csv("enriched.csv", parse_dates=["date"])
```

Now we select only the numeric vaccination fields:

```
metrics = [
    "daily_vaccinations",
    "total_vaccinations",
    "people_vaccinated",
    "people_fully_vaccinated"
```

```
]
data = df[metrics].dropna()
```

Computing Correlation Matrix

After this, we call pandas' correlation method:

```
corr = data.corr()
print(corr)
```

After running this, we can see a 4×4 table of correlation coefficients, where values near 1.0 indicate strong positive relationships.

Rendering Heatmap with 'imshow'

We then make use of **imshow** to visualize the matrix:

```
plt.figure(figsize=(6, 5))
plt.imshow(corr, interpolation="none", aspect="auto",
cmap="coolwarm")
plt.colorbar(label="Correlation Coefficient")
plt.xticks(range(len(metrics)), metrics, rotation=45,
ha="right")
plt.yticks(range(len(metrics)), metrics)
plt.title("Correlation Heatmap of Vaccination Metrics")
plt.tight_layout()
plt.show()
```

After running the above, our screen displays a colored grid where deep reds mark high positive correlations and blues indicate weaker links.

Interpreting Heatmap

Now in the resulted heatmap, a near-1.0 correlation between **total_vaccinations** and **people_vaccinated** confirms that cumulative doses and people with at least one shot rise together. A slightly lower correlation with **daily_vaccinations** suggests day-to-day counts fluctuate more independently. The relationship between **people_vaccinated** and **people_fully_vaccinated** reveals how quickly partial recipients become fully vaccinated.

This above heatmap equips us with a visual map of metric relationships, and it is going to be useful for feature selection and model design in the further recipes.

Pivot Tables

Now, although our dataset holds daily dose records, but yet we may desire to have a concise summary showing monthly totals per country. Manually grouping each combination takes time and risks errors. So here, we must use pandas' **`pivot_table`** to aggregate monthly sums by **`location`** and **`month`**, producing a clean table that compares countries at a glance.

Preparing Data for Pivoting

So, to begin with, we first open the **`pivot_table.py`** and import pandas and the loading of our cleaned data as we did in all the other previous recipes:

```
import pandas as pd
df = pd.read_csv("df_clean.csv", parse_dates=["date"])
df["month"] = df["date"].dt.to_period("M")
```

Now in the above, we specifically type the period in order to reduce the memory and to clarify the grouping by month.

Building Pivot Table

Here, we make a single call to **`pivot_table`** creates our summary:

```
monthly_pivot = pd.pivot_table(
    df,
    values="daily_vaccinations",
    index="location",
    columns="month",
    aggfunc="sum",
    fill_value=0
)
```

That yields a DataFrame where each row is a country, each column is a month, and each cell shows the total doses for that period.

Verifying and Inspecting Results

We then print the first few rows to confirm structure:

```
print(monthly_pivot.head(5))
```

Following is the expected output:

```
month                2020-02  2020-03  2020-04  2020-05  2020-
06  ...
location
Afghanistan                0        0        0     1500     2300
...
Albania                    0        0        0     5000     7200
...
Algeria                    0        0        0    10000    13000
...
Andorra                    0        0        0      800     1200
...
Angola                     0        0        0     3000     4500
...
```

After this, we can confirm that every country appears once and that missing months default to zero.

Pivot for Comparative Insights

In addition, we can do a quick transpose, such that it highlights countries in a given month:

```
print(monthly_pivot["2021-
06"].sort_values(ascending=False).head(10))
```

That lists the top ten countries by total vaccines in June 2021. We can also chart a few countries' trends:

```
subset = monthly_pivot.loc[["United States", "India",
"Brazil"], :]

subset.plot(kind="bar", stacked=True, figsize=(10, 6))
```

A stacked bar chart appears, showing how each country's monthly totals build up over time.

Overall, the pivot table now provides a powerful summary of monthly vaccination volumes by country.

Scatter-Matrix Plots

You have several numeric vaccination metrics—daily doses, totals, partial and full counts. But, let us say that we want to know how they interact pairwise. Now here, a scatter-matrix plot shows each variable plotted against every other, helping you spot clusters, linear relationships or outliers at a glance. So here, we need to generate one for **daily_vaccinations**, **total_vaccinations**, **people_vaccinated** and **people_fully_vaccinated**.

Let us understand first what a scatter matric plot is? It is basically a pair plot that arranges mini scatter plots in a grid. Each cell shows one variable on the x-axis and another on the y-axis. Diagonal cells often display histograms or density plots of a single variable. By viewing all pairs together, you can detect whether two metrics move in sync, form distinct clusters, or contain extreme values that merit investigation.

Now to begin with, we first open **scatter_matrix.py**, import pandas and matplotlibm, and then load our DataFrame with all vaccination columns:

```
import pandas as pd
import matplotlib.pyplot as plt
from pandas.plotting import scatter_matrix
df = pd.read_csv("enriched.csv", parse_dates=["date"])
```

We then select the numeric columns of interest:

```
features = [
    "daily_vaccinations",
    "total_vaccinations",
    "people_vaccinated",
    "people_fully_vaccinated"
]
data = df[features].dropna()
```

Generating Plot

Now here, we can make a single call to produce the matrix:

```
axes = scatter_matrix(
    data,
    figsize=(10, 10),
    diagonal="hist",
    alpha=0.5,
    marker="o",
    edgecolor="k"
)
```

We can then adjust the labels for readability:

```
for ax in axes.ravel():
    ax.set_xlabel(ax.get_xlabel(), rotation=45)
    ax.set_ylabel(ax.get_ylabel(), rotation=0)
```

And then finaly we can render:

```
plt.suptitle("Pairwise Relationships of Vaccination Metrics")
plt.tight_layout()
plt.show()
```

Interpreting Clusters, Trends and Outliers

After rendering, you will observe a very tight, upward-sloping clouds between **`total_vaccinations`** and **`people_vaccinated`**, confirming that cumulative doses and partial vaccination move together. A slightly wider spread appears in plots involving **`daily_vaccinations`**, indicating day-to-day volatility. The diagonal histograms reveal skewness in counts: a long right tail suggests occasional spikes. And, the outlier points far from the main cloud mark days or countries with extraordinary numbers, which you may later investigate or clip.

Time-Series Line Plots

We now come to the last recipe of this chapter. Now in this, lets say that we want to visualize how vaccination rollouts evolved over time for a handful of countries—perhaps to compare the pace of administration in the United States, India and Brazil. And, a simple table of numbers won't reveal trends or crossovers. So here, we need a time-series line chart that plots daily doses for each selected country on the same axes, with clear labels and styling so we can see which rollout climbed fastest or plateaued.

To proceed, we first open **time_series_plots.py** and begin with imports and data loading from the earlier recipe:

```
import pandas as pd
import matplotlib.pyplot as plt
df = pd.read_csv("df_clean.csv", parse_dates=["date"])
```

We then choose the countries you want to compare and filter the DataFrame:

```
countries = ["United States", "India", "Brazil"]
subset = df[df["location"].isin(countries)]
```

Pivoting for Line Plot

We then make a pivot, as it makes each country a separate column indexed by date:

```
ts = subset.pivot(
    index="date",
    columns="location",
    values="daily_vaccinations"
)
```

This yields a DataFrame where each column holds the time series for one country.

Plotting with pandas and Styling

Now to plot, we can simply create a line plot in one call and then adjust its styling:

```
ax = ts.plot(
    kind="line",
    figsize=(12, 6),
    linewidth=2,
    alpha=0.8
)
```

```
ax.set_title("Daily Vaccinations Over Time", pad=15)
ax.set_xlabel("Date", labelpad=10)
ax.set_ylabel("Daily Doses Administered", labelpad=10)
ax.legend(title="Country", loc="upper left")
plt.xticks(rotation=45)
plt.grid(True, linestyle="--", alpha=0.5)
plt.tight_layout()
plt.show()
```

In the above script,the **linewidth** and **alpha** primarily controls the line thickness and transparency. And the grid lines and rotated ticks are meant to improve the readability.

Now for the plot to appear, we run the following script:

```
python time_series_plots.py
```

This will display a multi-line chart where each colored line traces a country's daily vaccination counts. We can see surges, plateaus and dips at various dates. The differences in rollout speed become immediately obvious, guiding further analysis or annotation.

Summary

So in this chapter, we very well generated an overall summary of daily vaccination counts by calling **df.describe()**, which showed count, mean, median, quartiles and standard deviation. We then grouped it by country and computed custom aggregations—count, mean, median, standard deviation, minimum and maximum—so that we could compare central tendencies across nations. We extracted ISO week numbers and calculated average daily doses per week, revealing how global rollout rates climbed and dipped over time.

A histogram plot of **daily_vaccinations** clarified distribution shape, highlighted a right skew from occasional high-count days and identified the most common dose range. We then did compute a correlation matrix for **daily_vaccinations**, **total_vaccinations**, **people_vaccinated** and **people_fully_vaccinated**, then rendered it as a heatmap to visualize strong positive relationships and subtle differences among metrics. A pivot table aggregated monthly totals per country, producing a concise table that let us rank and compare vaccine volumes across periods. A scatter-matrix plot arranged pairwise scatter plots and diagonal histograms, helping us spot linear trends, clusters and outliers among key metrics.

And then lastly, we did illustrate the rollout trajectories of the time-series line plots for selected countries over time. This made it simple to see which nations accelerated or plateaued. Each of these techniques gave us a practical, hands-on insight into our cleaned vaccination dataset and prepared us for deeper modeling steps.

CHAPTER 4: OPTIMIZING DATA STRUCTURES AND PERFORMANCE

Overview

We now get into a new chapter. In this chapter, we try to get through and practice techniques. These techniques make data pipelines faster and leaner. First, we will vectorize calculations with NumPy to eliminate slow loops. Then, you will learn to convert string labels into Pandas categorical types for significant memory savings and consistent group-by results.

Next, we will demonstrate how to process huge CSV files in manageable chunks and how to map very large arrays to disk with memmap, ensuring that you never run out of memory. We will learn to set meaningful indices before joins, which makes merging millions of rows almost instantaneous. Finally, we will profile your pipeline's memory and speed with the built-in tools, and then we will apply precise optimizations that'll deliver significant performance gains. Ultimately, you will have a toolbox of methods to confidently scale your analyses as data volumes grow.

Vectorizing with NumPy

We now revisit to our scripts wherein we have written a loop to compute daily percentage changes in vaccinations for each country, but let us say that it crawled when applied to hundreds of thousands of rows. So here, we need a more efficient method that operates on entire arrays at once, so we can calculate day-over-day rates for every country in seconds instead of minutes.

To begin with, we first open **vectorize.py** together, and then we load and sort our data so that vaccination counts sit in chronological order by country.

```
import pandas as pd
import numpy as np
df = pd.read_csv("df_clean.csv", parse_dates=["date"])
df.sort_values(["location", "date"], inplace=True)
```

At this point, you have a DataFrame with daily counts neatly ordered. A pure-Python loop would fetch each row, compute a difference with its predecessor, divide by the previous value and append a result. Now here, a NumPy array, in contrast, performs that same difference and division in compiled code. We extract the entire column of daily counts as an array:

```
vals = df["daily_vaccinations"].to_numpy()
```

Now we allocate an array of identical length to hold our rate changes. We fill it briefly with **NaN** so that the first day per country remains undefined:

```
rate_arr = np.full_like(vals, fill_value=np.nan, dtype=float)
```

Next, we compute the difference between each day and its predecessor in one shot, then divide by the previous day's value wherever that value isn't zero. All of this happens in a single vector expression:

```
diff = vals[1:] - vals[:-1]

prev = vals[:-1]

rates = np.where(prev != 0, diff / prev, 0)

rate_arr[1:] = rates
```

We place our computed rates back into the DataFrame:

```
df["rate_change"] = rate_arr
```

A quick comparison of slice outputs confirms that our vectorized result matches what the loop would have produced, but finishes far more quickly. With this pattern, you accelerate rate calculations across all countries without changing any business logic—only by swapping loops for array operations.

Leveraging pandas Categorical Dtypes

You notice that the **location** column still uses object dtype, and your DataFrame's memory footprint remains tens of megabytes. Handling millions of rows with string labels stresses your system. We need to convert those labels into a categorical type so that each unique country name is stored once, cutting memory overhead dramatically.

You open **categorical_dtype.py** and begin by importing pandas:

```
import pandas as pd
```

Next, load your deduplicated DataFrame:

```
df = pd.read_csv("df_clean.csv", parse_dates=["date"])
```

You check memory usage of the **location** column before conversion:

```
mem_before = df["location"].memory_usage(deep=True)

print(f"Memory before: {mem_before:,} bytes")
```

The output might show something like:

```
Memory before: 7,200,000 bytes
```

That tells you how much space your string labels occupy.

Next, you then explain that converting to category replaces each label with a small integer code and a single lookup table of categories.

A one-line conversion applies that logic:

```
df["location"] = df["location"].astype("category")
```

We just wanted to let you know that this change happens in place and you don't have to repeat it in later recipes. We can measure memory usage again:

```
mem_after = df["location"].memory_usage(deep=True)
print(f"Memory after:  {mem_after:,} bytes")
```

The output may read as below:

```
Memory after:  1,200,000 bytes
```

This dramatic drop confirms that the categorical type cut memory by more than 80%. And, it looks like the way we group things hasn't changed.

```
grouped = df.groupby("location")["daily_vaccinations"].sum()
print(grouped.head(5))
```

If you observe it closely, there are identical aggregation results, showing no loss of functionality. This conversion not only accelerates operations that rely on integer codes but also keeps your workflows scalable as data grows.

Chunked File Processing

A loaded CSV file put our 8 GB of RAM to the test as the vaccination records grew into the millions. So, we need a way to read that file in manageable pieces, process each batch, then combine results. That way, we can calculate the total global doses without crashing the system.

To begin with, we create a new script, called as **chunked_processing.py** and access the CSV URL.

```
import pandas as pd
CSV_URL = (
    "https://github.com/owid/covid-19-data/"
    "raw/master/public/data/vaccinations/vaccinations.csv"
```

```
)
```

We then choose a chunk size that fits comfortably in memory—100 000 rows works well here.

```
chunk_size = 100_000
totals = []
```

Next, the loop goes through each chunk, filters out missing counts, limits it to entries from 2021, and adds up daily vaccinations by country.

```
for chunk in pd.read_csv(
    CSV_URL,
    usecols=["location", "date", "daily_vaccinations"],
    parse_dates=["date"],
    chunksize=chunk_size
):
    clean = chunk.dropna(subset=["daily_vaccinations"])
    recent = clean[clean["date"] >= "2021-01-01"]
    summary = (
        recent.groupby("location")["daily_vaccinations"]
        .sum()
        .reset_index()
    )
    totals.append(summary)
```

Now here, we do the concatenation and it pulls all partial summaries into one table:

```
combined = pd.concat(totals)
final_totals = (
    combined.groupby("location")["daily_vaccinations"]
    .sum()
    .reset_index()
)
```

We then print the top results to verify success:

```
print(final_totals.sort_values(
    by="daily_vaccinations", ascending=False
).head(10))
```

Once we run this script, then it ensures it does not load more than 100 000 rows at once. With this, our RAM stays stable while you compute global vaccination totals for 2021 onward.

Memory-Mapped Arrays

Now, there's an issue with the vaccination counts. We've converted those into a NumPy array and saved it to a binary file, but loading the whole thing on machines with limited RAM still crashes the session. We've got to work with datasets larger than memory by mapping the file to disk and reading only the portions we need on demand.

Converting Data to a Binary Array

So here, we begin in **memmap_arrays.py** by extracting our **daily_vaccinations** column and saving it as a **.npy** file:

```
import pandas as pd
import numpy as np
# Load cleaned data
df = pd.read_csv("df_clean.csv", parse_dates=["date"])
vals = df["daily_vaccinations"].to_numpy()
# Save to disk in NumPy's .npy format
np.save("vaccinations.npy", vals)
```

We can now have a file **vaccinations.npy** on disk. Rather than loading with **np.load**, we map it.

Loading with Memory Mapping

We then replace a full load with a memory-mapped load:

```
# mmap_mode='r' opens in read-only mode without loading into
RAM
```

```
vacc_mmap = np.load("vaccinations.npy", mmap_mode="r")
```

At this point, **vacc_mmap** behaves like a NumPy array but doesn't occupy RAM for all its elements—only the slices you access.

Inspecting File-backed Array

Next, we then quickly verify shape and dtype:

```
print("Shape:", vacc_mmap.shape)
print("Dtype:", vacc_mmap.dtype)
```

This gives us the confidence that the file has mapped correctly.

Performing Calculations

And if you want the global average daily vaccination without having to load everything, that's an option too. NumPy is pretty efficient, but it does things in a roundabout way. It reads chunks, but it doesn't do it all at once.

```
mean_val = vacc_mmap.mean()
print(f"Global mean daily vaccinations: {mean_val:.2f}")
```

Here, only the small blocks load at a time, keeping RAM usage minimal.

Creating Writable Memory Map

Next, if we need to update values in place like clipping the outliers directly on disk, we can open in read-write mode:

```
vacc_mmap_rw = np.memmap(
    "vaccinations.npy",
    dtype=vacc_mmap.dtype,
    mode="r+",
    shape=vacc_mmap.shape
)
# Clip values outside bounds directly on disk
lower, upper = 0, mean_val * 5
vacc_mmap_rw[:] = np.clip(vacc_mmap_rw, lower, upper)
```

```
vacc_mmap_rw.flush()  # ensure changes are written
```

Verifying Memory Efficiency

You monitor RAM while performing these steps and notice usage stays low even for multi-million–row arrays. Slicing still works as expected:

```
print(vacc_mmap[100000:100010])
```

That prints ten values without loading the full array.

With this, we are able to compute the statistics and even modify large arrays without ever exceeding system memory. This technique scales to datasets far larger than available RAM.

Efficient Joins via Indexing

After a good amount of time, our DataFrame with daily vaccination counts and population figures has grown to millions of rows. When we simply call **`pd.merge(vacc_df, pop_df, on=["location", "date"])`**, the operation grinds to a halt, chewing through RAM and CPU as it scans entire tables for each match. So here, we now need a way to speed up this join so that matching rows by country and date happens nearly instantaneously, even on large datasets.

To do this, we first open **`efficient_join.py`** together.

```
import pandas as pd
```

Now here, a quick load of both tables shows their raw state:

```
vacc_df = pd.read_csv("vacc_clean.csv", parse_dates=["date"])
pop_df  = pd.read_csv("pop_clean.csv")
```

By default, the pandas treats both **`location`** and **`date`** as regular columns, so every merge requires a costly lookup. We can teach pandas to use pre-built indices that function like ordered, hashed pointers into each row.

Setting Strong Indices

First, we tell pandas to index each DataFrame on the join keys:

```
vacc_df.set_index(["location", "date"], inplace=True)
pop_df.set_index(["location", "date"], inplace=True)
```

These multi-level indices allow pandas to locate matching rows via direct index alignment rather than full table scans. We explain that behind the scenes, pandas builds maps from each unique **(location, date)** pair to integer positions, so merges become pointer-based.

Performing Indexed Join

With indices in place, we call **join** instead of **merge**, leaning on index alignment:

```
joined_df = vacc_df.join(
    pop_df["population"],
    how="left",
    sort=False
)
```

Here, the **join** matches on each DataFrame's existing index. The **how="left"** parameter preserves every vaccination record, appending **population** where available. Setting **sort=False** avoids reordering, keeping the original chronological sequence.

Verifying Performance Gains

We measure time before and after:

```
import time
# Baseline merge
start = time.time()
_ = pd.merge(
    vacc_df.reset_index(),
    pop_df.reset_index(),
    on=["location", "date"],
    how="left"
)
print("Merge time:", time.time() - start)
# Indexed join
start = time.time()
_ = vacc_df.join(pop_df["population"], how="left", sort=False)
```

```
print("Indexed join time:", time.time() - start)
```

On large tables, the indexed join completes in a fraction of the merge time—often 5× to 10× faster.

Inspecting Joined DataFrame

We then run a quick check, which then confirms that the **population** is aligned correctly as below:

```
print(joined_df.head(5))
print(joined_df.info())
```

The sample output will then show that the rows are keyed by **(location, date)** with **daily_vaccinations** and **population** columns. By setting multi-level indices on our join keys, we turned a slow table scan into a rapid pointer lookup. This technique scales gracefully as datasets expand and becomes essential.

Profiling Operations

It seems like certain steps, like grouping by country or merging tables, are making our pipeline slow way down. We need a quick way to see which operations use the most memory and time so we can focus on what matters.

Inspecting Memory Usage

So here, we first do a check on how much memory our DataFrame uses before any heavy work. For this, we start an interactive IPython session in your **venv**:

```
ipython
```

Inside, we then import pandas and load the clean data:

```
In [1]: import pandas as pd
In [2]: df = pd.read_csv("df_clean.csv", parse_dates=["date"])
```

We then call **info** with **memory_usage='deep'** to see a detailed breakdown:

```
In [3]: df.info(memory_usage="deep")
<class 'pandas.core.frame.DataFrame'>
RangeIndex: 300000 entries, 0 to 299999
```

```
Data columns (total 5 columns):
 #   Column              Non-Null Count   Dtype
---  ------              --------------   -----
 0   location            300000 non-null  object
 1   date                300000 non-null  datetime64[ns]
 2   daily_vaccinations  300000 non-null  float64
 3   population          300000 non-null  int64
 4   rate_change         300000 non-null  float64
memory usage: 45.0 MB
```

After this, we see that **location** alone uses a large chunk of memory.

Timing Expensive Operations

Next, we then identify which operations take longest by using the **%timeit** magic:

```
In [4]: %timeit
df.groupby("location")["daily_vaccinations"].sum()
# 1 loop, best of 3: 250 ms per loop
```

We then measure a merge as well:

```
In [5]: pop = pd.read_csv("pop_clean.csv")
In [6]: %timeit df.merge(pop, on=["location"], how="left")
# 1 loop, best of 3: 400 ms per loop
```

The grouping and merging each took a few hundred milliseconds on your machine.

Profile-based Optimizing

Since the **location** appears costly, we try to convert it to a categorical type and re-measure:

```
In [7]: df["location"] = df["location"].astype("category")
In [8]: df.info(memory_usage="deep")
# memory usage: 10.5 MB
In [9]: %timeit
df.groupby("location")["daily_vaccinations"].sum()
```

```
# 10 loops, best of 3: 30 ms per loop
In [10]: %timeit df.merge(pop, on=["location"], how="left")
# 10 loops, best of 3: 80 ms per loop
```

If we observe closely the output, the memory usage drops by over 50%, and group-by and merge speed up by roughly 8× and 5× respectively.

With this, we have now learned to pinpoint bottlenecks with **`df.info(memory_usage='deep')`** and **`%timeit`**, and to apply targeted optimizations—such as converting columns to categorical—to achieve dramatic performance gains across your data pipeline.

Summary

Overall, in this chapter, we successfully replaced slow Python loops with NumPy bulk operations to compute day-over-day rate changes across all countries in seconds. We then converted our **`location`** column into a categorical type, slashing memory usage by over 80% while preserving accurate grouping. We read massive CSVs in fixed-size chunks, filtered and aggregated each batch to calculate global vaccination totals without ever exhausting RAM.

Next, we mapped large binary arrays to disk with NumPy's **`memmap`**, letting us compute means and clip outliers on datasets far bigger than available memory. We set multi-level indices on **`location`** and **`date`** before joining vaccination and population tables, turning costly table scans into near-instant pointer lookups. Finally, we spotted performance hotspots with **`df.info(memory_usage='deep')`** and **`%timeit`**, then applied targeted fixes such as categorical conversion, which then helped us to speed up group-by and merge operations by up to tenfold.

Chapter 5: Feature Engineering and Transformation

Overview

We have now reached the halfway point of this book. Here, we will explore techniques that enrich and transform features to create more powerful models. We will start by creating polynomial and interaction terms to capture nonlinear relationships in vaccination data. Then, you will compare the MinMax, standard, and robust scaling strategies to understand how each one affects the distributions of features.

Next, we will use a seven-day moving average to smooth daily fluctuations and highlight long-term rollout patterns. Then, we will apply principal component analysis to collapse multiple features into a few components that retain most of the variance, which makes visualization and clustering easier. Finally, we will cover how to efficiently encode high-cardinality categorical variables using one-hot encoding in a sparse format and integrate those sparse features into a machine learning pipeline.

Creating Polynomial Features

Right now, our models use just basic vaccination metrics. They might miss interactions, like the days when a really high daily dose and high per-capita rates together show a fast rollout. We want to add some complexity to your data using squared terms and cross-products so that simple linear models can capture nonlinear effects.

We open a new script named **`poly_features.py`** and load the libraries and the dataframe.

```
vim poly_features.py
import pandas as pd
from sklearn.preprocessing import PolynomialFeatures
df = pd.read_csv("df_clean.csv", parse_dates=["date"])
# assume per_capita_scaled already exists from previous
recipes
```

We then extract the two columns we want to expand:

```
X = df[["daily_vaccinations", "per_capita_scaled"]]
```

After this, we create a **`PolynomialFeatures`** instance for degree 2 (squared and interaction terms) without adding a constant bias column:

```
poly = PolynomialFeatures(degree=2, include_bias=False)
X_poly = poly.fit_transform(X)
```

Next, we then generate human-readable feature names and build a new DataFrame:

```
feature_names =
poly.get_feature_names_out(input_features=["daily_vaccinations
", "per_capita_scaled"])

poly_df = pd.DataFrame(X_poly, columns=feature_names,
index=df.index)
```

We then combine these new columns with your original data:

```
df_expanded = pd.concat([df, poly_df], axis=1)
```

Just make sure the squared and interaction terms are in the right place.

```
print(df_expanded[feature_names].head(5))

print(f"Original features: {X.shape[1]}, Expanded features:
{X_poly.shape[1]}")

python poly_features.py
```

It will yield something like:

```
daily_vaccinations  per_capita_scaled  daily_vaccinations^2
daily_vaccinations per_capita_scaled  per_capita_scaled^2

0                0.0               -1.23               0.00
-0.00               1.51

1                0.0               -1.22               0.00
-0.00               1.49

2                0.0               -1.20               0.00
-0.00               1.44

3                0.0               -1.19               0.00
-0.00               1.42

4                0.0               -1.18               0.00
-0.00               1.39

Original features: 2, Expanded features: 5
```

With this, we have now squared versions of **daily_vaccinations** and **per_capita_scaled**, plus their interaction term. These enriched features can feed directly into regression or classification models, helping capture nonlinear relationships without complex custom code.

Scaling Strategies Compared

As you can see in the models, there's sensitivity to feature scales. A few large vaccination values had a big impact, while small per-capita figures barely influenced the results. We want to compare different scaling methods—MinMax, Standard, and Robust—to see which one gives us balanced distributions before feeding features into a model.

For this, we create a script named **compare_scalers.py** with relevant libraries loaded and the dataset as well:

```
import pandas as pd
from sklearn.preprocessing import MinMaxScaler,
StandardScaler, RobustScaler
df = pd.read_csv("df_clean.csv", parse_dates=["date"])
X = df[["daily_vaccinations"]]
```

Then, instantiate each scaler and fit-transform the data.

```
scalers = {
    "minmax": MinMaxScaler(),
    "standard": StandardScaler(),
    "robust": RobustScaler()
}
scaled = {}
for name, scaler in scalers.items():
    scaled[name] = scaler.fit_transform(X)
```

Next, we create a comparison table showing key statistics for each scaled feature:

```
comparison = pd.DataFrame({
    name: pd.Series(vals.flatten()).describe()
    for name, vals in scaled.items()
})
print(comparison.T)
```

Following is what we might see:

```
              count        mean          std    min      25%      50%      75%
max
minmax   300000.0   0.5000   0.3500  0.0    0.200  0.500  0.800
1.0
standard300000.0   0.0000   1.0000 -1.10 -0.700  0.000  0.700
2.50
robust 300000.0   0.0500   0.9000 -0.85 -0.300  0.050  0.400
3.00
```

As you know, the MinMaxScaler squeezes values into the range of [0,1]. StandardScaler centers on zero with unit variance, and RobustScaler uses the median and interquartile range to reduce the influence of outliers.

To see the effects of each change on the distribution, just add a quick histogram for each.

```
import matplotlib.pyplot as plt
for name, vals in scaled.items():
    pd.Series(vals.flatten()).hist(bins=50)
    plt.title(f"{name.capitalize()} Scaled Distribution")
    plt.xlabel("Scaled Value")
    plt.ylabel("Frequency")
    plt.show()
```

If you look closely, you'll see that MinMax gives uniform spread, Standard keeps a Gaussian shape centered on zero, and Robust compresses extreme values more gently. With these insights, you can choose the scaling method that best suits your downstream model's robustness and performance.

Computing Rolling Aggregates

The daily numbers of vaccinations being administered are all over the place, making it tough to spot any real trends. We want to smooth that noise by averaging each day's value with the six days before it. The seven-day moving average shows underlying patterns, like sustained increases or plateaus, without needing to do manual calculations.

So here, we open a **rolling_aggregates.py** together with the DataFrame:

```
import pandas as pd
```

```
df = pd.read_csv("df_clean.csv", parse_dates=["date"])
```

Now here, a sort by country and date ensures that each rolling window covers consecutive days:

```
df.sort_values(["location", "date"], inplace=True)
```

We can compute the seven-day average on **daily_vaccinations** grouped by country:

```
df["weekly_avg"] = (
    df
    .groupby("location")["daily_vaccinations"]
    .transform(lambda x: x.rolling(window=7,
min_periods=1).mean())
)
```

The above code processes each country's time series independently, filling the first six days with the average of available prior days.

Later, we can run a quick check that shows the new column in action:

```
print(df.loc[df["location"] == "United States", ["date",
"daily_vaccinations", "weekly_avg"]].head(10))
```

Following is something you will see as an output:

```
        date  daily_vaccinations  weekly_avg
0  2020-12-01               10000   10000.000
1  2020-12-02               12000   11000.000
2  2020-12-03               11000   11000.000
3  2020-12-04               13000   11500.000
4  2020-12-05               14000   12000.000
5  2020-12-06               12500   12083.333
6  2020-12-07               13500   12500.000
7  2020-12-08               15000   13214.286
8  2020-12-09               14500   13857.143
9  2020-12-10               16000   14214.286
```

Finally, to visualize the smoothed trend, we can plot both raw and averaged series:

```
import matplotlib.pyplot as plt
subset = df[df["location"] == "United States"].set_index("date")
ax = subset[["daily_vaccinations", "weekly_avg"]].plot(
    figsize=(12, 6),
    alpha=0.8
)
ax.set_title("Daily vs 7-Day Average Vaccinations (United States)")
ax.set_xlabel("Date")
ax.set_ylabel("Doses Administered")
plt.tight_layout()
plt.show()
```

The resulting line chart highlights how weekly averages remove short-term spikes, clarifying long-term rollout patterns.

With this, we have now explored to apply rolling window functions to smooth noisy time series data. This technique makes trend detection and model inputs far more reliable.

Principal Component Analysis

Now so far, we have worked with multiple scaled vaccination features—**daily_vaccinations**, **per_capita_scaled** and possibly polynomial terms—but high dimensionality hinders visualization and may introduce noise. So here, we need to apply PCA so that we capture most variance in just two or three components, simplifying downstream modeling and insight discovery.

To do this, we open **pca_reduction.py** with the libraries and the PCA class:

```
vim pca_reduction.py
import pandas as pd
from sklearn.decomposition import PCA
```

Next, we then load our DataFrame as usual. Now here, we have already created the scaled features in earlier recipes and concatenated them into a CSV named **df_features.csv**:

```
df = pd.read_csv("df_features.csv", parse_dates=["date"])
```

First, we select the numeric feature columns to reduce, for example:

```
features = [
    "daily_vaccinations",
    "per_capita_scaled",
    "daily_vaccinations^2",
    "per_capita_scaled^2",
    "daily_vaccinations per_capita_scaled"
]
X = df[features]
```

Then we instantiate the PCA to retain enough components to explain 90% of the variance:

```
pca = PCA(n_components=0.90, random_state=42)
X_pca = pca.fit_transform(X)
```

We then retrieve the number of components chosen and the explained variance ratio:

```
n_comp = pca.n_components_
var_ratio = pca.explained_variance_ratio_.cumsum()
print(f"Number of components: {n_comp}")
print("Cumulative explained variance by component:")
for i, ratio in enumerate(var_ratio, start=1):
    print(f" Component {i}: {ratio:.2%}")
```

The output may look like:

```
Number of components: 2
Component 1: 85.30%
Component 2: 98.75%
```

The above output tells us that two principal components capture almost all variance.

Next, we then create a new DataFrame for these components alongside the original index:

```
pca_df = pd.DataFrame(
    X_pca,
    columns=[f"PC{i}" for i in range(1, n_comp+1)],
    index=df.index
)
df_reduced = pd.concat([df, pca_df], axis=1)
```

We then verify the new DataFrame structure:

```
print(df_reduced[["PC1", "PC2"]].head(5))
```

The sample output will be like this:

```
       PC1        PC2
0 -1.23456   0.12345
1 -1.21098   0.09876
2 -1.18543   0.07654
3 -1.16012   0.05432
4 -1.13457   0.03210
```

Then plot the first two components to visualize clusters or trends:

```
import matplotlib.pyplot as plt
plt.scatter(df_reduced["PC1"], df_reduced["PC2"], alpha=0.5,
s=10)
plt.title("PCA Projection of Vaccination Features")
plt.xlabel("Principal Component 1")
plt.ylabel("Principal Component 2")
plt.tight_layout()
plt.show()
```

After running this, a scatter plot appears, showing how countries or dates cluster in reduced space. With this, we have now reduced multiple vaccination features down to a handful of principal components that capture nearly all variability.

One-Hot Encoding High-Cardinality

Our **location** column holds hundreds of unique country names. If we naively encode each with a separate binary column, our feature set balloons and memory usage soars. So here, we need a way to transform these high-cardinality categories into a machine-learning–friendly format without exhausting RAM.

For this, first we open a new script called **onehot_encoding.py** and start by importing pandas and loading the DataFrame:

```
import pandas as pd
df = pd.read_csv("df_clean.csv", parse_dates=["date"])
df["location"] = df["location"].astype("category")
```

We then run a quick memory check. It shows our starting point:

```
before = df["location"].memory_usage(deep=True)
print(f"Location column memory: {before:,} bytes")
```

Generating Sparse One-Hot Columns

Now for this, we call **get_dummies** with **sparse=True**, which returns a sparse DataFrame:

```
dummies = pd.get_dummies(
    df["location"],
    prefix="loc",
    sparse=True,
    dtype=int
)
```

This creates one column per country but stores it efficiently. We inspect its memory:

```
after = dummies.memory_usage(deep=True).sum()
print(f"Sparse one-hot memory: {after:,} bytes")
```

We can then see a dramatic drop compared to a dense representation.

Integrating with Feature Matrix

Here, we concatenate the sparse dummies alongside numeric features for modeling:

```
features = pd.concat(
    [df[["daily_vaccinations", "per_capita_scaled"]],
dummies],
    axis=1
)
```

Now here, the **features** is a sparse-aware DataFrame. We confirm its format:

```
print(features.info())
```

Converting to SciPy Sparse Matrix

It is very well known that many ML libraries accept the SciPy sparse input. We export our sparse DataFrame to COO format:

```
sparse_matrix = features.sparse.to_coo().tocsr()
print(type(sparse_matrix), sparse_matrix.shape)
```

That yields a **csr_matrix** with one row per record and one column per feature, stored compactly in memory.

And finally, as a final check, we plug this sparse matrix into a scikit-learn pipeline step without error:

```
from sklearn.linear_model import LogisticRegression
model = LogisticRegression(max_iter=100)
model.fit(sparse_matrix, (df["daily_vaccinations"] >
0).astype(int))
```

We can see training proceed without swapping to dense arrays, confirming that our one-hot encoding scales to high-cardinality without blowing out RAM.

Summary

In summary, we used scikit-learn's **PolynomialFeatures** to create the interactions and squared terms from our vaccination metrics. This allowed the simple models to capture nonlinear effects. We applied three scaling strategies—**MinMaxScaler**, **StandardScaler**, and **RobustScaler**—and compared their impact on feature distributions to determine the most suitable transformation. We smoothed daily noise by computing seven-day rolling averages with the rolling method in Pandas, which revealed clearer trends over time.

Then, we reduced the dimensionality with PCA, retaining two components that explained over 90 percent of the variance in our scaled features. Finally, we visualized the resulting clusters. Finally, we transformed hundreds of country labels into a sparse, one-hot format using pandas's **`get_dummies`**, which we then converted into a SciPy CSR matrix. This enabled our machine learning pipelines to handle high cardinality without exhausting memory.

CHAPTER 6: BUILDING MACHINE LEARNING PIPELINES

Overview

Here in this chapter, we will learn to package every preprocessing and modeling step into a single, maintainable pipeline. We will learn to define end-to-end pipelines that handle imputation, scaling and model fitting with one command. Next, you will create custom transformer classes to encapsulate domain logic—such as date feature extraction and missing-value strategies—so that your code remains DRY and flexible. We will then apply automated hyperparameter tuning with **GridSearchCV**, exploring parameter combinations under cross-validation to find the best model settings.

After training, you will learn to persist and reload the entire pipeline using **joblib**, guaranteeing identical behavior across environments. And then, you will integrate feature selection within your pipeline by leveraging **SelectKBest**, enabling automatic selection of the most informative vaccination features before fitting. By doing all this, we will be able to strengthen our practical ability to design robust and scalable machine learning workflows.

End-to-End Pipelines

Let us think of a challenge wherein we have stitched together the imputation, scaling and model fitting in separate steps, but switching between them feels error-prone when you tweak features or try new estimators. So here, we need a single object that bundles all preprocessing and modeling into one call, so that you can train and predict in one line and swap components without rewriting code.

For this, we first open **pipeline_end_to_end.py** with the as usual imports:

```
vim pipeline_end_to_end.py
import pandas as pd
from sklearn.pipeline import Pipeline
from sklearn.impute import SimpleImputer
from sklearn.preprocessing import StandardScaler
from sklearn.linear_model import Ridge
```

Next, we then load our feature matrix and target. Here, we can predict per-capita scaled vaccination as a regression example:

```
df = pd.read_csv("df_features.csv", parse_dates=["date"])
X = df[["daily_vaccinations", "daily_vaccinations^2"]]
y = df["per_capita_scaled"]
```

We then define a pipeline that first fills missing values with the median, then standardizes every feature, then fits a Ridge regressor:

```
pipeline = Pipeline([
    ("imputer", SimpleImputer(strategy="median")),
    ("scaler", StandardScaler()),
    ("model", Ridge(alpha=1.0, random_state=42))
])
```

We can get the training happenning in one call:

```
pipeline.fit(X, y)
```

We also can inspect the trained model's coefficients immediately:

```
coefs = pipeline.named_steps["model"].coef_
print("Coefficients:", coefs)
```

And when you predict on new or held-out data, it also reduces to one line. If you saved a test split as **`X_test`**, you'd write:

```
preds = pipeline.predict(X_test)
```

That single object handles imputation, scaling and regression under the hood. We avoid mistakes from forgetting a transform step, and you can swap in a different estimator—say **`RandomForestRegressor()`**—by changing only the pipeline definition.

With this end-to-end pipeline, our workflow becomes concise and modular. We can use the same pattern in classification tasks or more complex feature assemblies, ensuring that every step runs reliably in sequence.

Custom Transformer Classes

Since our workflow involves encoding **`date`** features like year, month, and weekday, and handling missing values before scaling, it's important to keep those elements in mind. Putting that logic in for every dataset muddies our code and invites mistakes. We need transformers that we can reuse and that plug into any pipeline. That way, we can call each step by name and swap in new logic without rewriting preprocessing code.

We create a new file named **`custom_transformers.py`** with the required libs:

```
vim custom_transformers.py
from sklearn.base import BaseEstimator, TransformerMixin
import pandas as pd
```

Creating DateEncoder Transformer

We then define a transformer that reads a DataFrame with a **date** column and appends **year**, **month** and **weekday** features:

```
class DateEncoder(BaseEstimator, TransformerMixin):
    def __init__(self, date_column="date"):
        self.date_column = date_column
    def fit(self, X, y=None):
        return self
    def transform(self, X):
        X_copy = X.copy()
        X_copy[self.date_column] =
pd.to_datetime(X_copy[self.date_column])
        X_copy["year"]    = X_copy[self.date_column].dt.year
        X_copy["month"]   = X_copy[self.date_column].dt.month
        X_copy["weekday"] =
X_copy[self.date_column].dt.dayofweek
        return X_copy.drop(columns=[self.date_column])
```

We then explain that **fit** simply returns **self**, since no learning occurs, and **transform** handles both date parsing and feature extraction.

Creating MedianImputer Transformer

Next, we encapsulate missing-value logic for numeric columns:

```
class MedianImputer(BaseEstimator, TransformerMixin):
    def __init__(self, columns=None):
        self.columns = columns
        self.medians_ = {}
```

```
    def fit(self, X, y=None):
        data = X if self.columns is None else X[self.columns]
        self.medians_ = data.median().to_dict()
        return self
    def transform(self, X):
        X_copy = X.copy()
        for col, med in self.medians_.items():
            X_copy[col].fillna(med, inplace=True)
        return X_copy
```

That transformer computes and stores medians during **fit**, then fills missing entries in **transform**.

Using Transformers in Pipeline

Here, we show how to chain these with scaling and modeling:

```
from sklearn.pipeline import Pipeline
from sklearn.preprocessing import StandardScaler
from sklearn.linear_model import Ridge
pipeline = Pipeline([
    ("date_encode", DateEncoder(date_column="date")),
    ("impute", MedianImputer(columns=["daily_vaccinations"])),
    ("scale", StandardScaler()),
    ("model", Ridge())
])
```

Verifying Transformer Behavior

To inspect the output, we load a sample DataFrame and run the pipeline up to **scale**:

```
import pandas as pd
df = pd.read_csv("df_clean.csv", parse_dates=["date"])
processed = pipeline.named_steps["date_encode"].transform(df)
```

```
processed =
pipeline.named_steps["impute"].transform(processed)
print(processed[["year", "month", "weekday",
"daily_vaccinations"]].head())
```

From the above script, the sample output shows new temporal columns and no missing values:

```
  year  month  weekday  daily_vaccinations
0  2020      2        5             10000.0
1  2020      2        6             12000.0
2  2020      2        0             11000.0
3  2020      2        1             13000.0
4  2020      2        2             14000.0
```

With these custom transformers, you can encapsulate domain-specific preprocessing and plug them into any machine learning pipeline, improving code clarity and reusability.

Hyperparameter Tuning

Let us see some other challenge. Assume that our pipeline imputes, scales and fits a Ridge model, but default settings may not yield the best predictions. And the manually adjusting the regularization strength or other parameters feels like guesswork. So here, we need an automated way to search across parameter combinations with cross-validation, so that we can identify the optimal settings and measure their performance reliably.

For this, first we open **tune_hyperparams.py** with the required libraries:

```
vim tune_hyperparams.py
import pandas as pd
from sklearn.pipeline import Pipeline
from sklearn.impute import SimpleImputer
from sklearn.preprocessing import StandardScaler
from sklearn.linear_model import Ridge
from sklearn.model_selection import GridSearchCV,
train_test_split
from sklearn.metrics import mean_squared_error
```

Next, we then load our features and target, and split into training and hold-out sets:

```
df = pd.read_csv("df_features.csv", parse_dates=["date"])
X = df[["daily_vaccinations", "daily_vaccinations^2"]]
y = df["per_capita_scaled"]
X_train, X_test, y_train, y_test = train_test_split(
    X, y, test_size=0.2, random_state=42
)
```

We then define a pipeline that handles missing values, scaling and regression:

```
pipeline = Pipeline([
    ("impute", SimpleImputer(strategy="median")),
    ("scale", StandardScaler()),
    ("model", Ridge())
])
```

Here, a parameter grid lists the **`alpha`** values to try for Ridge:

```
param_grid = {
    "model__alpha": [0.01, 0.1, 1.0, 10.0, 100.0]
}
```

We then set up **`GridSearchCV`** with 5-fold cross-validation and negative mean squared error as our scoring metric:

```
grid = GridSearchCV(
    pipeline,
    param_grid,
    cv=5,
    scoring="neg_mean_squared_error",
    n_jobs=-1
)
```

We then kick off the search by fitting on the training data:

```
grid.fit(X_train, y_train)
```

If we try to get a printed summary, it may reveal the best **alpha** and its corresponding score:

```
print("Best alpha:", grid.best_params_["model__alpha"])
print("Best CV MSE:", -grid.best_score_)
```

After this, we then evaluate on the hold-out set to confirm generalization:

```
preds = grid.predict(X_test)
mse_test = mean_squared_error(y_test, preds)
print("Test set MSE:", mse_test)
```

the sample run might display:

```
Best alpha: 1.0
Best CV MSE: 0.035
Test set MSE: 0.038
```

This will tell us that **alpha=1.0** balanced bias and variance best across folds, and produced solid performance on unseen data. By wrapping everything in **GridSearchCV**, you automated hyperparameter selection and obtained reliable performance estimates without manual tweaking.

Pipeline Persistence

You've tuned and trained a complex pipeline that imputes values, scales features and fits a regression model. Each time you restart your script or switch machines, you must retrain from scratch—wasting time and risking inconsistencies between batch and real-time inference. We must save the entire pipeline in its trained state so that we can reload it later and call **predict** immediately, guaranteeing identical behavior in every environment.

We first open **persist_pipeline.py** together.

```
vim persist_pipeline.py
```

Then, we import what we need:

```
import pandas as pd
import joblib
```

```
from sklearn.pipeline import Pipeline
from sklearn.impute import SimpleImputer
from sklearn.preprocessing import StandardScaler
from sklearn.linear_model import Ridge
```

Next, load and split your data—replicating the setup you used originally:

```
df = pd.read_csv("df_features.csv", parse_dates=["date"])
X = df[["daily_vaccinations", "daily_vaccinations^2"]]
y = df["per_capita_scaled"]
```

We then define and train the pipeline exactly as before:

```
pipeline = Pipeline([
    ("impute", SimpleImputer(strategy="median")),
    ("scale", StandardScaler()),
    ("model", Ridge(alpha=1.0, random_state=42))
])
pipeline.fit(X, y)
```

Now we persist the trained object to disk with joblib:

```
joblib.dump(pipeline, "vaccination_pipeline.joblib")
print("Pipeline saved to vaccination_pipeline.joblib")
```

Here, the message confirms that the entire pipeline—including fitted imputer, scaler parameters and model coefficients—resides in one file.

After this, in a new Python session or production script, you simply load and predict:

```
import joblib
import pandas as pd
# reload the pipeline
loaded_pipeline = joblib.load("vaccination_pipeline.joblib")
# prepare new data (or reuse X from before)
new_X = pd.read_csv("new_data.csv", parse_dates=["date"])[
```

```
    ["daily_vaccinations", "daily_vaccinations^2"]
]
# immediate prediction without retraining
predictions = loaded_pipeline.predict(new_X)
print(predictions[:5])
```

That one-line load ensures that batch jobs and real-time services share the same preprocessing logic and model weights. No drift, no retraining errors—just consistent, instant inference.

Feature Selection within Pipelines

There are dozens of features we have generated, like raw metrics, polynomial terms, and per-capita rates. But training on all of them slows down model fitting and risks overfitting. Picking the best features manually each time feels tedious. We want our pipeline to automatically select the top K vaccination-related features before fitting, so that model training focuses on the most informative inputs without extra scripting.

To begin with, we open a new file called **select_kbest_pipeline.py**. with the as usual libraries:

```
nano select_kbest_pipeline.py
import pandas as pd
from sklearn.feature_selection import SelectKBest,
f_regression
from sklearn.preprocessing import StandardScaler
from sklearn.linear_model import Ridge
from sklearn.pipeline import Pipeline
```

Next, we then load your feature data. We assume you exported all candidate features (including squared and interaction terms) in **df_expanded.csv** with a target column **per_capita_scaled**:

```
df = pd.read_csv("df_expanded.csv", parse_dates=["date"])
X = df.drop(columns=["date", "per_capita_scaled"])
y = df["per_capita_scaled"]
```

We then decide to keep the top 5 features based on univariate F-tests. A pipeline defines selection, scaling and regression:

```
pipeline = Pipeline([
    ("select", SelectKBest(score_func=f_regression, k=5)),
    ("scale", StandardScaler()),
    ("model", Ridge(alpha=1.0, random_state=42))
])
```

After this, we fit the pipeline on your full data:

```
pipeline.fit(X, y)
```

Now here, to see which features were chosen, we extract the boolean mask and map it back to column names:

```
mask = pipeline.named_steps["select"].get_support()
selected_features = X.columns[mask].tolist()
print("Selected features:", selected_features)
```

This will print something like as below:

```
Selected features: ['daily_vaccinations', 'per_capita_scaled',
'daily_vaccinations^2', 'PC1', 'PC2']
```

Finally, we then perform a quick cross-validation to confirm that using only those features does not degrade performance:

```
from sklearn.model_selection import cross_val_score
scores = cross_val_score(
    pipeline, X, y, cv=5, scoring="neg_mean_squared_error",
n_jobs=-1
)
print("CV MSE scores:", -scores)
print("Average CV MSE:", -scores.mean())
```

With thhis, we can see consistent error rates, showing that the pipeline's built-in selection step streamlines feature choice without manual filtering. By integrating **SelectKBest** into your pipeline, you automate feature selection and ensure that every model fit uses only the top predictors. That saves you time and keeps your workflow concise and maintainable.

Summary

Overall, we built an end-to-end pipeline that imputes missing values, scales features, and trains a Ridge regression with one call. This simplifies our workflow and reduces errors from manual step chaining. We encapsulated date encoding and median imputation in custom transformers by subclassing **`BaseEstimator`** and **`TransformerMixin`**, which made those steps reusable and clear. We then automated hyperparameter tuning with **`GridSearchCV`**.

Next, we persisted the trained pipeline using **`joblib's`** dump and load functions, ensuring consistent batch and real-time inference without the need for retraining. We integrated feature selection directly into our pipeline using **`SelectKBest`** with an F-test to allow for the automatic identification of the top predictors before model fitting. Each recipe in this chapter reinforced assembling, tuning, and deploying robust, modular workflows in scikit-learn. This whole chapter taught us how we can easily move our vaccination data smoothly from raw inputs to predictions with minimal boilerplate and maximal reproducibility.

CHAPTER 7: IMPLEMENTING STATISTICAL AND MACHINE LEARNING TECHNIQUES

Overview

This chapter will address the challenges associated with rigorous statistical testing and machine learning methods on vaccination data. First, we will apply t-tests and chi-square tests to determine if there are significant differences in daily rates and high-coverage events across regions. Next, you will learn to train and interpret linear and Ridge regression models in order to quantify the impact of demographic and rate-change predictors on per-capita uptake. Then, we will introduce tree-based learners, such as decision trees and random forests, to capture nonlinear patterns and extract feature importances.

Next, we will cover clustering algorithms, which will allow you to segment countries by rollout behavior using K-means and hierarchical methods. We will learn to evaluate each model using the appropriate metrics: mean squared error and R^2 for regression accuracy, classification reports for precision and recall, and ROC curves with AUC for classifier performance. By the end of this chapter, you will have a toolbox of statistical and machine learning approaches to uncover, validate, and predict vaccination trends.

Hypothesis Testing

You want to know whether vaccination rates differ significantly between two regions—say, Europe and Asia. Manual eyeballing of averages feels inadequate. We must apply a t-test to compare mean daily vaccinations and a chi-square test to examine whether high-coverage days occur more often in one region versus another.

To begin with, we first open **hypothesis_tests.py**, import libraries and load the cleaned DataFrame:

```
import pandas as pd
from scipy.stats import ttest_ind, chi2_contingency
df = pd.read_csv("df_clean_with_region.csv",
parse_dates=["date"])
```

Performing Two-Sample t-Test

We then extract daily vaccination arrays for Europe and Asia:

```
europe = df[df["region"] ==
"Europe"]["daily_vaccinations"].dropna()
asia   = df[df["region"] ==
"Asia"]["daily_vaccinations"].dropna()
```

We just say that t.test shows if the two means are different.

```
t_stat, p_val = ttest_ind(europe, asia, equal_var=False)
print(f"t-statistic: {t_stat:.3f}, p-value: {p_val:.3e}")
```

Here, the p-value below 0.05 suggests significant difference in average daily rates.

Conducting Chi-Square Test

We categorize each day as "high" if daily vaccinations exceed the overall median:

```
median_val = df["daily_vaccinations"].median()
df["high_coverage"] = df["daily_vaccinations"] > median_val
```

A contingency table counts high vs low days per region:

```
ct = pd.crosstab(df["region"], df["high_coverage"])
print(ct)
```

That might show:

```
high_coverage   False   True
region
Asia             80000  70000
Europe           60000  90000
```

Then we apply **chi2_contingency** to test independence:

```
chi2, p, dof, _ = chi2_contingency(ct)
print(f"chi2: {chi2:.2f}, p-value: {p:.3e}, dof: {dof}")
```

Now here, the low p-value indicates that high-coverage days are not equally likely in both regions.

With this, we have now applied both t-test and chi-square test to assess differences in vaccination patterns across regions. These statistical methods guide you in choosing appropriate modeling strategies or in flagging regional disparities for deeper investigation.

Regression Models

So far, we have built features such as **per_capita** and demographic predictors like

population and growth rate, but we need to quantify how those factors drive vaccination uptake. A simple linear model can reveal which predictors matter most, while Ridge regression helps prevent overfitting when predictors correlate. We will train both models on our data and interpret their coefficients to gain actionable insight.

To begin with, we first open the **regression_models.py** and load the data.

```
vim regression_models.py
import pandas as pd
from sklearn.model_selection import train_test_split
from sklearn.linear_model import LinearRegression, Ridge
from sklearn.metrics import mean_squared_error, r2_score
df = pd.read_csv("df_clean.csv", parse_dates=["date"])
```

We can have a quick glance shows that **df** contains **per_capita** (doses per 100 people), **population**, and our previously computed **rate_change**:

```
print(df[["per_capita", "population", "rate_change"]].head(5))
```

The output might read:

```
  per_capita  population  rate_change
0     0.012345     38928346          NaN
1     0.015678     38928346     0.270270
2     0.014321     38928346    -0.086419
3     0.017810     38928346     0.243902
4     0.019876     38928346     0.115702
```

We then drop the first row to eliminate the NaN in **rate_change**:

```
df = df.dropna(subset=["rate_change"])
```

Next, we select our predictor matrix **X** and target vector **y**:

```
X = df[["population", "rate_change"]]
y = df["per_capita"]
```

We split into training and test sets for honest evaluation:

```
X_train, X_test, y_train, y_test = train_test_split(
    X, y, test_size=0.2, random_state=42
)
```

Training Linear Regression

Now here we must know that a linear model fits coefficients by minimizing squared error. So here, we instantiate and fit:

```
linreg = LinearRegression()
linreg.fit(X_train, y_train)
```

We then print learned coefficients and intercept:

```
print("Linear Regression intercept:", linreg.intercept_)
print("Coefficients:", dict(zip(X.columns, linreg.coef_)))
```

Following is the expected output:

```
Linear Regression intercept: 0.005123
Coefficients: {'population': 1.23e-10, 'rate_change': 0.0456}
```

We then interpret that every unit increase in **rate_change** adds roughly 0.0456 to per-capita dose rate, while **population** has a very small coefficient, suggesting its effect scales with other factors.

Evaluating Linear Model

The predictions and metrics primarily reveal the fit quality:

```
y_pred = linreg.predict(X_test)
print("Linear MSE:", mean_squared_error(y_test, y_pred))
print("Linear R2:", r2_score(y_test, y_pred))
```

So here, we might see:

```
Linear MSE: 0.000123
Linear R2: 0.72
```

An R^2 of 0.72 indicates that 72% of per-capita variance is explained by our two predictors.

Training Ridge Regression

The ridge adds L2 penalty to shrink coefficients and reduce overfitting when features correlate. In this, we fit with α=1.0:

```
ridge = Ridge(alpha=1.0, random_state=42)
ridge.fit(X_train, y_train)
print("Ridge coefficients:", dict(zip(X.columns,
ridge.coef_)))
```

Here, we can notice slightly smaller coefficient magnitudes compared to LinearRegression, reflecting regularization.

Evaluating Ridge Model

We then check Ridge performance on the test set:

```
y_pred_r = ridge.predict(X_test)
print("Ridge MSE:", mean_squared_error(y_test, y_pred_r))
print("Ridge R2:", r2_score(y_test, y_pred_r))
```

If Ridge R^2 is similar or slightly higher, it confirms that regularization helped.

We used both LinearRegression and Ridge to figure out how to model relationships between per-capita vaccination and demographic predictors. Interpreting the coefficients showed the impact of each feature, and comparing performance metrics showed if regularization improved generalization.

Tree-Based Methods

We have seen linear and regularized models but found that they struggle to capture complex, nonlinear relationships in vaccination patterns—such as thresholds or interaction effects that don't follow straight lines. We need models that adapt flexibly to data shapes, split on feature values automatically, and reveal which variables drive those splits. Decision trees and random forests fit that need, letting us learn nonlinear patterns and extract feature importances without manual feature engineering.

To begin with, we first open **`tree_models.py`** and bring up the tree-based regressors, along with utilities for splitting and evaluation:

```
vim tree_models.py
import pandas as pd
from sklearn.model_selection import train_test_split
from sklearn.tree import DecisionTreeRegressor
from sklearn.ensemble import RandomForestRegressor
from sklearn.metrics import mean_squared_error, r2_score
```

Next, we then load the cleaned and the last used DataFrame that already contains numeric features such as **daily_vaccinations**, **per_capita_scaled**, **rate_change** and **weekly_avg**:

```
df = pd.read_csv("df_clean.csv", parse_dates=["date"])
df["weekly_avg"] = (
    df.groupby("location")["daily_vaccinations"]
      .transform(lambda x: x.rolling(window=7,
min_periods=1).mean())
)
```

Preparing Features and Target

We select the four predictors that Tree-based models handle naturally without scaling:

```
X = df[[
    "daily_vaccinations",
    "per_capita_scaled",
    "rate_change",
    "weekly_avg"
]]
y = df["per_capita_scaled"]
```

A train–test split reserves 20 percent of data for evaluation:

```
X_train, X_test, y_train, y_test = train_test_split(
    X, y, test_size=0.2, random_state=42
```

```
)
```

Training Decision Tree Regressor

We instantiate a tree with limited depth to avoid overfitting—depth 5 balances flexibility with interpretability:

```
tree = DecisionTreeRegressor(max_depth=5, random_state=42)
tree.fit(X_train, y_train)
```

A single decision tree learns splits such as "if daily_vaccinations > 10 000 then …" that capture nonlinear thresholds in data.

Evaluating Tree

We predict on our test set and compute performance:

```
y_pred_tree = tree.predict(X_test)
mse_tree = mean_squared_error(y_test, y_pred_tree)
r2_tree  = r2_score(y_test, y_pred_tree)
print(f"Decision Tree - MSE: {mse_tree:.6f}, R²:
{r2_tree:.3f}")
```

An R^2 closer to 1.0 indicates that the tree captures complex patterns better than linear models.

Inspecting Feature Importances

The **DecisionTreeRegressor** exposes **feature_importances_**, showing how much each split criterion reduced impurity:

```
importances = tree.feature_importances_
feature_names = X.columns
for name, imp in zip(feature_names, importances):
    print(f"{name}: {imp:.3f}")
```

Here, a high importance for **weekly_avg** or **rate_change** tells us that those nonlinear patterns matter most when predicting per-capita vaccination rates.

Training Random Forest Regressor

A single tree can overfit despite depth limits. A RandomForestRegressor builds an ensemble of many trees on random subsets of data and features, averaging their predictions for robust, nonlinear modeling:

```
forest = RandomForestRegressor(
    n_estimators=100,
    max_depth=5,
    random_state=42,
    n_jobs=-1
)
forest.fit(X_train, y_train)
```

Evaluating Forest

We predict with the forest and compare metrics:

```
y_pred_forest = forest.predict(X_test)
mse_forest = mean_squared_error(y_test, y_pred_forest)
r2_forest  = r2_score(y_test, y_pred_forest)
print(f"Random Forest - MSE: {mse_forest:.6f}, R²:
{r2_forest:.3f}")
```

Often the forest improves R^2 and lowers MSE, demonstrating its power to capture subtler nonlinear trends without manual tuning of feature interactions.

Averaging Feature Importances

We then extract and average importances across all trees:

```
importances_forest = forest.feature_importances_
for name, imp in zip(feature_names, importances_forest):
    print(f"{name}: {imp:.3f}")
```

When you compare the importance of a tree versus a forest, you can see which predictors always lead to accurate results.

Visualizing a Single Tree (Optional)

To see how splits occur, you can plot one tree from the forest:

```
from sklearn.tree import plot_tree
import matplotlib.pyplot as plt
plt.figure(figsize=(12, 8))
plot_tree(
    forest.estimators_[0],
    feature_names=feature_names,
    filled=True,
    max_depth=3,
    fontsize=8
)
plt.show()
```

From the plot diagram, you can explore the decision rules like "if rate_change ≤ 0.2 then … else …" illustrating how the model partitions data. We can observe that trees capture regimes—periods when daily vaccinations exceed certain thresholds lead to markedly higher per-capita rates. Forest importances highlight which metrics matter most across varied conditions. Unlike linear models, tree-based methods adapt to nonlinearities without explicit interaction terms.

Clustering Algorithms

We want to group countries by how their vaccination campaigns progressed—identifying fast adopters versus slow starters. Manually inspecting each country's stats is tedious. We must apply clustering to segment nations based on features like average daily doses and per-capita uptake, so that patterns emerge automatically.

We open **clustering.py**, import pandas, clustering tools and a scaler to prepare our features:

```
vim clustering.py
import pandas as pd
from sklearn.preprocessing import StandardScaler
from sklearn.cluster import KMeans, AgglomerativeClustering
import matplotlib.pyplot as plt
```

We then load our cleaned dataset and compute country-level summaries:

```
df = pd.read_csv("df_clean.csv", parse_dates=["date"])
summary = (
    df.groupby("location")
      .agg(
          avg_daily=("daily_vaccinations", "mean"),
          avg_weekly=("weekly_avg", "mean"),
          per_capita_mean=("per_capita", "mean")
      )
      .reset_index()
)
```

A quick look at **summary.head()** shows three numeric features for each country.

```
print(summary.head())
```

We then extract those features into **X** and standardize them so that clustering isn't dominated by scale differences:

```
features = ["avg_daily", "avg_weekly", "per_capita_mean"]
X = summary[features]
scaler = StandardScaler()
X_scaled = scaler.fit_transform(X)
```

K-Means Clustering

We choose four clusters as a starting point.

```
kmeans = KMeans(n_clusters=4, random_state=42)
kmeans_labels = kmeans.fit_predict(X_scaled)
summary["kmeans_cluster"] = kmeans_labels
```

We inspect cluster centers in original feature space by reversing scaling:

```
centers = scaler.inverse_transform(kmeans.cluster_centers_)
centers_df = pd.DataFrame(centers, columns=features)
```

```
print("Cluster centers:\n", centers_df)
```

A scatter plot of two features reveals distinct groupings:

```
plt.figure(figsize=(8,6))
for cluster in range(4):
    mask = summary["kmeans_cluster"] == cluster
    plt.scatter(
        summary.loc[mask, "avg_daily"],
        summary.loc[mask, "per_capita_mean"],
        label=f"Cluster {cluster}",
        alpha=0.7
    )
plt.xlabel("Average Daily Vaccinations")
plt.ylabel("Average Per-Capita Vaccinations")
plt.legend()
plt.title("KMeans Clusters of Countries")
plt.tight_layout()
plt.show()
```

Agglomerative Clustering

We can take a hierarchical approach which can reveal nested group structures.

```
agg = AgglomerativeClustering(n_clusters=4, linkage="ward")
summary["agg_cluster"] = agg.fit_predict(X_scaled)
```

We then compare cluster assignments between methods:

```
comparison = summary.groupby(["kmeans_cluster",
"agg_cluster"]).size()
print("Cluster assignment overlap:\n", comparison)
```

This gives a table that shows how many countries share the same labels under both methods. With this, we have now segmented countries into clusters based on vaccination rollout characteristics. Here, the KMeans gave us centroids to interpret average behavior, while AgglomerativeClustering highlighted hierarchical groupings. These clusters can guide targeted policy analysis or further modeling tailored to different country groups.

Model Evaluation Metrics

We've used regression and classification algorithms to predict vaccination outcomes, but we're not sure how well they work. A simple accuracy score doesn't show if your regression errors stay small or if your classification models handle imbalanced classes right. We need some solid metrics—like mean squared error for regression, precision/recall reports for classification, and ROC curves for classifier discrimination—to gauge the model's quality and make improvements.

Regression Evaluation with MSE

We begin by loading your regression model and test data. In **evaluate_regression.py**, import libraries and reload your saved pipeline or model:

```
import pandas as pd
import joblib
from sklearn.metrics import mean_squared_error, r2_score
# reload pipeline trained to predict per_capita_scaled
pipeline = joblib.load("vaccination_pipeline.joblib")
# load test set prepared earlier
df = pd.read_csv("df_features.csv", parse_dates=["date"])
X = df[["daily_vaccinations", "daily_vaccinations^2"]]
y = df["per_capita_scaled"]
# split or load previous split; for reproducibility we split again
from sklearn.model_selection import train_test_split
X_train, X_test, y_train, y_test = train_test_split(
    X, y, test_size=0.2, random_state=42
)
```

A single call computes predictions on the hold-out set:

```
y_pred = pipeline.predict(X_test)
```

We then calculate the mean squared error and R^2:

```
mse = mean_squared_error(y_test, y_pred)
r2  = r2_score(y_test, y_pred)
print(f"Mean Squared Error: {mse:.6f}")
print(f"R² Score          : {r2:.4f}")
```

Following is the expected sample output:

```
Mean Squared Error: 0.032150
R² Score          : 0.7542
```

These values tell you that average squared deviation between predicted and actual per-capita rates is 0.032. An R^2 of 0.75 indicates that 75 percent of variance is explained by your model.

You can inspect error distribution to identify systematic bias:

```
import matplotlib.pyplot as plt
errors = y_test - y_pred
plt.hist(errors, bins=50, edgecolor="black")
plt.title("Distribution of Prediction Errors")
plt.xlabel("Error (Actual - Predicted)")
plt.ylabel("Frequency")
plt.tight_layout()
plt.show()
```

If the histogram is centered and symmetrical, it means the errors are unbiased. Long tails suggest some occasional big misses, which you could deal with using nonlinear models or feature augmentation.

Classification Evaluation with Precision, Recall and ROC Curve

We move on to figuring out how to classify things. One example is trying to predict if a country will reach a certain number of vaccinations for each person (like more than 50 doses per 100 people). We prepare a binary target:

```
# continue in evaluate_regression.py or open
evaluate_classification.py
```

```
from sklearn.linear_model import LogisticRegression
from sklearn.metrics import classification_report, roc_curve,
auc
# define binary target
df["high_coverage"] = (df["per_capita"] > 50).astype(int)
# select features for classification
X_cls = df[["daily_vaccinations", "per_capita_scaled",
"rate_change"]]
y_cls = df["high_coverage"]
Xc_train, Xc_test, yc_train, yc_test = train_test_split(
    X_cls, y_cls, test_size=0.2, random_state=42
)
# train a logistic regression
clf = LogisticRegression(solver="liblinear", random_state=42)
clf.fit(Xc_train, yc_train)
```

We can then have a classification report that summarizes precision, recall and F1-score:

```
yc_pred = clf.predict(Xc_test)
report = classification_report(yc_test, yc_pred,
target_names=["Low", "High"])
print(report)
```

You may expect a similar output like this:

```
              precision    recall  f1-score   support
         Low       0.82      0.88      0.85     12000
        High       0.80      0.72      0.76      8000
    accuracy                           0.81     20000
   macro avg       0.81      0.80      0.80     20000
weighted avg       0.81      0.81      0.81     20000
```

Here, we can then observe that precision for the "High" class is 0.80, meaning 80 percent of predicted high-coverage cases were correct. Recall of 0.72 indicates that 72 percent of actual high-coverage days were identified.

Drawing ROC Curve

We then compute the predicted probabilities and ROC metrics:

```
# probability of positive class
y_prob = clf.predict_proba(Xc_test)[:, 1]
fpr, tpr, thresholds = roc_curve(yc_test, y_prob)
roc_auc = auc(fpr, tpr)
# plot ROC
plt.figure(figsize=(6, 6))
plt.plot(fpr, tpr, label=f"AUC = {roc_auc:.3f}", linewidth=2)
plt.plot([0, 1], [0, 1], linestyle="--", color="gray")
plt.title("ROC Curve for High Coverage Classifier")
plt.xlabel("False Positive Rate")
plt.ylabel("True Positive Rate")
plt.legend(loc="lower right")
plt.tight_layout()
plt.show()
```

Here, the AUC above 0.80 shows strong discrimination ability. We adjust thresholds based on desired trade-offs; for example, a threshold that yields a higher true positive rate at the cost of more false positives.

Comparing Multiple Models

After this, we wrap the evaluation into a reusable function to compare classifiers:

```
def evaluate_classifier(model, X_train, X_test, y_train,
y_test):
    model.fit(X_train, y_train)
    y_pred = model.predict(X_test)
    print(classification_report(y_test, y_pred))
    y_prob = model.predict_proba(X_test)[:, 1]
```

```
    fpr, tpr, _ = roc_curve(y_test, y_prob)
    print(f"AUC: {auc(fpr, tpr):.3f}")
    plt.plot(fpr, tpr, label=type(model).__name__)
plt.figure(figsize=(6, 6))
evaluate_classifier(LogisticRegression(solver="liblinear"),
Xc_train, Xc_test, yc_train, yc_test)
evaluate_classifier(RandomForestRegressor(random_state=42),
Xc_train, Xc_test, yc_train, yc_test)  # use classifier here
plt.plot([0, 1], [0, 1], "--", color="gray")
plt.title("ROC Comparison")
plt.xlabel("False Positive Rate")
plt.ylabel("True Positive Rate")
plt.legend()
plt.tight_layout()
plt.show()
```

It's as easy as switching models, and you can compare performance right on the same plot.

You've used mean squared error and R^2 to check the performance of the regression, used classification reports and ROC curves for binary predictions, and built evaluation routines that can be reused. With these metrics, you can measure the strengths and weaknesses of the models, adjust the thresholds to fit real-world needs, and pick the best algorithm for each task of predicting vaccinations.

Summary

In short, we successfully applied a two-sample t-test to compare the mean daily number of vaccinations in Europe and Asia. Then, we used a chi-square test on a contingency table of high-coverage days to confirm regional differences. We trained a linear regression model and a ridge regressor on population and rate-change predictors. We then inspected their coefficients and evaluated performance using mean squared error (MSE) and R^2. We found that regularization improved generalization.

Next, we moved to flexible, tree-based methods—**DecisionTreeRegressor** and **RandomForestRegressor**—training each on raw and derived features. We measured their **MSE** and **R^2** and extracted feature importances to highlight which vaccination metrics drove predictions. Then, we segmented countries by vaccination rollout characteristics using K-means and agglomerative clustering on average daily doses, weekly averages, and per capita uptake. After that, we visualized the clusters and compared the assignments.

Ultimately, we developed robust evaluation routines: mean squared error and R^2 for regression; classification report for precision and recall in binary high-coverage prediction; and ROC curves with AUC to evaluate classifier discrimination. We can compare multiple models using the same metrics thanks to reusable functions. All of these techniques provided concrete evidence of model validity, guided feature choices, and revealed actionable insights into vaccination patterns.

Chapter 8: Debugging and Troubleshooting

Overview

Here, in this chapter, we explore and get hands-on with the common debugging and troubleshooting techniques for key Python data-science libraries. We will first learn how to diagnose and resolve merge conflicts in pandas by inspecting _merge indicators, aligning data types and cleaning whitespace so that tables join without missing rows.

Next, you will tackle NumPy broadcasting errors by checking array shapes, reshaping vectors into the correct dimensions and understanding how broadcasting rules apply to row- and column-wise operations. We will then see how to ensure consistent visual output with matplotlib by selecting an appropriate backend, setting global figure dimensions and DPI, and using savefig options for identical plots in notebooks and scripts.

Finally, you will discover how to track memory leaks during long-running loops using **memory_profiler**, and how to clear references and trigger garbage collection to prevent RAM bloat. By the chapter's end, you will have a toolbox of diagnostic steps and practical fixes that keep your data pipelines robust, reproducible and performant.

Resolving pandas Merge Errors

We tried to join our vaccination DataFrame with a population table using **pd.merge**, yet the result has missing matches and unexpected row counts. We notice mismatched keys—perhaps one column is integer, the other string, or extra whitespace sneaks into country names. We need to inspect key types and index alignment, then fix those mismatches so that every country's vaccination counts align correctly with its population data.

Inspecting Merge Behavior

Let's reproduce the issue in a script named **merge_debug.py**. We start by loading both tables:

```
import pandas as pd

vacc = pd.read_csv("vacc_clean.csv", parse_dates=["date"])

pop   = pd.read_csv("pop_clean.csv")
```

We then try to merge:

```
merged = pd.merge(

    vacc,

    pop,

    on=["location"],
```

```
    how="left",
    indicator=True
)
print(merged["_merge"].value_counts())
```

The **_merge** column reveals how many rows came from both tables versus left-only or right-only. A high count of **left_only** means many vaccination rows found no population match.

Checking Key Dtypes and Whitespace

We now inspect dtypes and a sample of unique labels:

```
print(vacc["location"].dtype, pop["location"].dtype)
print(vacc["location"].unique()[:5])
print(pop["location"].unique()[:5])
```

If one shows **object** and the other **category**, or if names like **"United States "** (trailing space) appear, those mismatches cause merge failures.

Cleaning Key Columns

We then decide to standardize both columns by stripping whitespace and casting to string:

```
for df in (vacc, pop):
    df["location"] = df["location"].astype(str).str.strip()
```

If dtypes differ, you enforce the same:

```
vacc["location"] = vacc["location"].astype("category")
pop["location"]  = pop["location"].astype("category")
```

Aligning Categories If Categorical

When using categorical dtype, we need to ensure both share the same categories:

```
common =
sorted(set(vacc["location"]).intersection(pop["location"]))
cat_type = pd.api.types.CategoricalDtype(categories=common)
vacc["location"] = vacc["location"].astype(cat_type)
```

```
pop["location"]  = pop["location"].astype(cat_type)
```

Performing Corrected Merge

With keys cleaned and aligned, rerun the merge:

```
merged = pd.merge(
    vacc,
    pop,
    on="location",
    how="left",
    indicator=True
)
print(merged["_merge"].value_counts())
```

By now, we should see all rows under **both** and only a handful **left_only** for truly missing population entries.

Verifying Clean Join

We now drop the indicator and confirm no missing population values where you expect both:

```
merged = merged.drop(columns="_merge")
missing_pop = merged["population"].isna().sum()
print(f"Rows with missing population after fix: {missing_pop}")
```

A zero or minimal count confirms that **location** keys now match perfectly. After checking the merge indicators, unifying dtypes, getting rid of extra whitespace, and aligning the categorical domains, we got the vaccination and population tables to merge cleanly and reliably.

Correcting NumPy Broadcasting

We tried to crunch the numbers to figure out the rate changes for each country by multiplying a 1-D array of country-level factors with a 2-D array of daily vaccination counts, but we got a "shape mismatch" error from NumPy. First, we have to check the array shapes, and then we'll reshape one of the arrays so that the rows line up with the countries when we do the broadcasting, and we don't have any problems.

Reproducing Broadcasting Error

We need to open **broadcast_debug.py** and load pandas and NumPy:

```
import pandas as pd
import numpy as np
df = pd.read_csv("df_clean.csv", parse_dates=["date"])
df.sort_values(["location", "date"], inplace=True)
```

We then extract a 2-D array of daily counts, grouped by country (each row for one country, each column for a day):

```
countries = df["location"].unique()
daily_matrix = np.array([
    df[df["location"] == loc]["daily_vaccinations"].to_numpy()
    for loc in countries
])
print("daily_matrix shape:", daily_matrix.shape)
```

Now here, suppose we have a per-country scaling factor in a 1-D array:

```
factors = np.random.rand(len(countries))
print("factors shape     :", factors.shape)
```

The best is to attempt to apply scaling directly fails:

```
scaled = daily_matrix * factors
# ValueError: operands could not be broadcast together with
shapes (200,1500) (200,)
```

Inspecting Shapes and Reasoning

We then print both shapes:

```
daily_matrix shape: (200, 1500)
factors shape     : (200,)
```

We can have the NumPy try to align trailing dimensions:

- First array: (200, 1500)
- Second : (200,)

The rows match the number of countries (200), but there are 1,500 daily columns, so we need a matching factor for each column, not each row.

Explicit Reshaping for Correct Broadcasting

We reshape **factors** into a column vector so that each factor multiplies its country's entire row:

```
factors_col = factors.reshape(-1, 1)  # shape (200,1)
print("factors_col shape:", factors_col.shape)
```

Now broadcasting rules align:

- (200,1500)
- (200,1)

The NumPy expands the second dimension across 1500 columns automatically.

Applying Fixed Broadcast

We then compute scaled matrix without error:

```
scaled = daily_matrix * factors_col
print("scaled shape       :", scaled.shape)
```

Following is the expected output:

```
scaled shape       : (200, 1500)
```

A simple check as below shows that each country's first-day value is multiplied by its factor:

```
country0_vals = daily_matrix[0, :5]
country0_scaled = scaled[0, :5]
print("Original  :", country0_vals)
print("Factor    :", factors[0])
print("Scaled    :", country0_scaled)
```

Here, you then observe that **scaled[i, j] == daily_matrix[i, j] * factors[i]** holds for every entry.

By checking shapes and reshaping the factor array into a column vector, you avoided NumPy broadcasting errors and made sure that each country's entire time series was scaled right. This pattern is used whenever a 1-D array has to multiply rows or columns of a 2-D array without dimension mismatches.

Matplotlib Rendering Fixes

Our charts look fine in notebooks, but when we run the same script from the terminal, the figures get smaller or the axes overlap. We need consistent visuals when plotting interactively or saving files. First, we'll need to set the figure size and resolution. We'll also need to choose a backend that works well with both Jupyter and standalone scripts so that every plot renders the same way in each.

So here, we create **render_fixes.py**.

```
vim render_fixes.py
```

We then specify a non-interactive backend—**Agg** works for PNG output in scripts:

```
import matplotlib
matplotlib.use("Agg")  # use a non-GUI backend for scripts
```

Next, we import pyplot and adjust global settings:

```
import matplotlib.pyplot as plt
# Set default figure size and DPI for all plots
plt.rcParams["figure.figsize"] = (10, 6)
plt.rcParams["figure.dpi"]     = 150
```

This will explain that **rcParams** applies to every figure, ensuring consistency without repeating parameters.

Generating Test Plot

Now here, we load the sample data and produce a line chart:

```
import numpy as np
# Dummy vaccination rollout for demonstration
days = np.arange(1, 31)
vaccines = np.random.randint(1000, 5000, size=30)
```

```
plt.plot(days, vaccines, linewidth=2, marker="o", alpha=0.8)
plt.title("Test Vaccination Trend")
plt.xlabel("Day of Month")
plt.ylabel("Doses Administered")
plt.grid(True, linestyle="--", alpha=0.5)
plt.tight_layout()
plt.savefig("vaccination_trend.png")
# plt.show()  # optional, but no display when using Agg
python render_fixes.py
```

After running the script, we can then inspect **vaccination_trend.png**. It should match your notebook's appearance exactly.

If you require higher resolution for a presentation, then we can override DPI:

```
plt.savefig("vaccination_trend_hd.png", dpi=300)
```

This produces a 300-dpi image without changing global settings.

Switching Backends in Notebooks

When you return to Jupyter, reset to the inline backend for interactive viewing:

```
import matplotlib
matplotlib.use("module://ipykernel.pylab.backend_inline")
```

Or simply start cells with **%matplotlib inline** to restore default behavior.

By fixing the backend to **Agg** in scripts, setting **figure.figsize** and **figure.dpi** via **rcParams**, and using **savefig** with explicit DPI, you guarantee that every chart looks the same whether you plot in a notebook or run a standalone script.

Tracking Memory Leaks

Even though our chunked processing loop worked, the RAM usage climbed steadily after dozens of iterations until the notebook crashed. We need to figure out where memory builds up and free up unused objects so that long-running pipelines stay stable.

So here, we open a new script called **track_memory.py**.

```
vim track_memory.py
```

Installing 'memory_profiler'

We first install the profiler:

```
pip install memory_profiler
```

This brings in the **@profile** decorator and **memory_usage** function. No further installs will be required.

Profiling a Function

We then import tools and write a sample processing function:

```
import pandas as pd
from memory_profiler import memory_usage
import gc
CSV_URL = (
    "https://github.com/owid/covid-19-data/"
    "raw/master/public/data/vaccinations/vaccinations.csv"
)
def process_chunk(chunk):
    # simulate some work
    result = chunk.dropna(subset=["daily_vaccinations"])
    summary = result["daily_vaccinations"].sum()
    return summary
def run_pipeline():
    totals = []
    for chunk in pd.read_csv(
        CSV_URL,
        usecols=["location", "date", "daily_vaccinations"],
        parse_dates=["date"],
        chunksize=100000
```

```
    ):
        totals.append(process_chunk(chunk))
        # clear references and collect garbage
        del chunk
        gc.collect()
    return sum(totals)
```

We can then decorate **run_pipeline** to measure line-by-line memory:

```
@profile
def run_and_profile():
    total = run_pipeline()
    print(f"Total vaccinations since 2021: {total}")
mprof run track_memory.py
mprof plot
```

After running the above, a memory-usage graph appears over time. We can then look over it for steady upward trends that signal leaks.

Clearing Object References

Here, we can notice memory spikes after each chunk. A reminder that **del chunk** and **gc.collect()** inside the loop ensure no leftover references. If you had created intermediate DataFrames or large arrays, you'd **del** them as well:

```
# inside loop
intermediate = chunk[chunk["location"] == "USA"]
# process...
del intermediate
gc.collect()
```

Measuring with 'memory_usage'

For more control, we can call **memory_usage** around code blocks:

```
from memory_profiler import memory_usage
```

```
mem_before = memory_usage()[0]
result = run_pipeline()
mem_after  = memory_usage()[0]
print(f"Memory before: {mem_before} MiB, after: {mem_after}
MiB")
```

Here, if there is a minimal increase, it then confirms that your cleanup worked.

With this, we have now learned to pinpoint memory leaks with **memory_profiler**, clear object references, and force garbage collection so that iterative processing loops run stably without gradual RAM bloat.

Summary

To quickly summarize what we learned, here we inspected merge failures by adding an **_merge** indicator and discovered that mismatched key types and stray whitespace in **location** columns prevented proper joins. We standardized those keys by stripping spaces and aligning categorical domains before rerunning **pd.merge**, which yielded complete matches. We debugged NumPy broadcasting errors by printing array shapes, realizing that a (n,) factor array needed reshaping to (n,1) so that row-wise multiplication would broadcast correctly.

Next, we fixed inconsistent plot renderings across environments by setting the **Agg** backend in scripts, configuring **figure.figsize** and **dpi** via **rcParams**, and using **savefig** with explicit DPI to guarantee identical output in both Jupyter and standalone scripts. We identified memory leaks in iterative processing loops by profiling with **memory_profiler**, then inserted **del** statements for temporary DataFrames and called **gc.collect()** to release unused objects. Through these recipes, we transformed vague errors into systematic inspections of dtypes, shapes, backends and memory usage, applying targeted fixes that restored reliability and performance in our pandas, NumPy and matplotlib workflows.

CHAPTER 9: ADVANCED DATA RETRIEVAL AND INTEGRATION

Overview

This is our final chapter. It takes us through advanced techniques for retrieving and integrating data from multiple external systems. First, you will schedule automated API pulls to update your vaccination datasets regularly.

After that, you will connect to MongoDB and use PyMongo to consume document-based metadata, merging it with existing CSV records to enrich your tables. Then, you will learn how to offload large files to Amazon S3 and Google Cloud Storage programmatically and retrieve them as needed within your Python scripts. We will also set up Kafka consumers to ingest real-time vaccination streams and align them with historical batch snapshots in Pandas. This will allow you to maintain a single, coherent DataFrame over time. We will implement robust retry and exponential backoff logic around your HTTP requests to handle rate limits and network hiccups gracefully.

Finally, you will use GraphQL queries with requests, change the nested responses into flat tables, and mix them with REST-based data. This makes hybrid datasets that use the strengths of both APIs. By the end of this chapter, you will have built a fully automated, resilient data pipeline that can handle diverse sources and formats with minimal manual effort.

Scheduling API Pulls

It'd be great if our vaccination data frame could be kept up to date without having to do manual downloads. Getting the CSV daily by hand is a pain and full of mistakes. We want an automated task that pulls the latest data at a regular interval—like every morning at 8:00—so that our analyses always use fresh records.

So again, we create a script called **scheduled_fetch.py** and install the lightweight **schedule** library:

```
vim scheduled_fetch.py
pip install schedule
```

This brings in the scheduling functions we need. Future recipes will assume it's available.

Writing Fetch Job

In **scheduled_fetch.py**, we start by importing libraries and defining the URL:

```
import pandas as pd
import schedule
import time
```

```
CSV_URL = (
    "https://github.com/owid/covid-19-data/"
    "raw/master/public/data/vaccinations/vaccinations.csv"
)
```

We then define a function that fetches and saves the CSV locally:

```
def fetch_latest():
    df = pd.read_csv(
        CSV_URL,
        usecols=["location", "date", "daily_vaccinations"],
        parse_dates=["date"]
    )
    df.to_csv("latest_vaccinations.csv", index=False)
    print("Fetched and saved latest data:",
pd.Timestamp.now())
```

Scheduling Job

Snow we schedule **fetch_latest** to run each day at 08:00:

```
schedule.every().day.at("08:00").do(fetch_latest)
```

If we prefer every hour for more frequent updates, we then use:

```
schedule.every().hour.do(fetch_latest)
```

Running Scheduler Loop

We then add a loop that keeps the script alive and checks for pending tasks:

```
if __name__ == "__main__":
    print("Scheduler started. Waiting for next fetch...")
    fetch_latest()  # initial run
    while True:
        schedule.run_pending()
```

```
    time.sleep(60)  # check every minute
```

Starting Scheduler

After this, we run the script in a dedicated terminal or as a background process:

```
python scheduled_fetch.py &
```

We can see an initial fetch immediately, followed by daily updates at 08:00. Each run writes **latest_vaccinations.csv**, ensuring your pipeline always reads the freshest data. With this setup, you no longer worry about stale inputs. Your analysis scripts can simply load **latest_vaccinations.csv**, confident that it reflects the most recent data.

NoSQL Data Access

There might be a situation where our vaccination CSV doesn't have rich metadata, like region codes or special attributes, stored in a MongoDB collection. It's a pain having to export documents manually and convert them to CSV, especially when it messes with our workflow. We need code that connects to MongoDB, fetches the vaccination metadata as documents, converts them to a DataFrame, and merges that with your existing CSV records for a unified view.

Installing PyMongo

To install, we then run one command in our active virtual environment:

```
pip install pymongo python-dotenv
```

This brings in the MongoDB driver and dotenv support. No further installation steps for these libraries will follow.

Storing MongoDB Credentials

In our project root, we then create or update a **.env** file (never commit this) with:

```
MONGO_URI=mongodb+srv://username:password@cluster0.mongodb.net
/mydb?retryWrites=true&w=majority
```

Writing MongoDB-Access Script

First, we open **nosql_access.py** in your editor and start with imports:

```
import os
```

```
from dotenv import load_dotenv
import pandas as pd
from pymongo import MongoClient
```

We then load environment variables and connect:

```
load_dotenv()
uri = os.getenv("MONGO_URI")
if not uri:
    raise RuntimeError("MONGO_URI must be set in .env")
client = MongoClient(uri)
db = client["covid_db"]
meta_coll = db["vaccination_metadata"]
```

Fetching Documents and Creating DataFrame

We then query all metadata documents, selecting only the fields you need—**`location`**, **`country_code`** and **`continent`**:

```
cursor = meta_coll.find(
    {},
    {"_id": 0, "location": 1, "country_code": 1, "continent":
1}
)
meta_list = list(cursor)
meta_df = pd.DataFrame(meta_list)
print(meta_df.head())
```

Loading Existing CSV Records

After this, we load our main CSV of daily counts as before:

```
vacc_df = pd.read_csv(
    "latest_vaccinations.csv",
    parse_dates=["date"]
```

```
)
```

Merging NoSQL Metadata with CSV Data

If we do the merge on **location**, it will enrich each daily record with its code and continent:

```
enriched = pd.merge(
    vacc_df,
    meta_df,
    on="location",
    how="left"
)
print(enriched.head())
print("Rows without metadata:",
enriched["country_code"].isna().sum())
```

With this, we confirm that every **location** now carries **country_code** and **continent** where available.

Verifying and Saving Results

A final info check ensures dtypes and non-null counts:

```
print(enriched.info())
enriched.to_csv("vacc_with_metadata.csv", index=False)
print("Enriched data saved to vacc_with_metadata.csv")
```

We've now integrated document-based metadata from MongoDB into your pandas workflow, joining it with CSV records to produce a rich, unified dataset.

Cloud Storage Integration

We might want to store and retrieve large vaccination CSVs or model artifacts in the cloud so that our local disk stays clean and your data pipelines run in distributed environments. It's a pain to do manual uploads via browser because they're slow and you can't expand them. We need code that can upload files to Amazon S3 or Google Cloud Storage (GCS) and download them when needed, all within the same Python workflow.

Installing Cloud Clients

We first install both clients:

```
pip install boto3 google-cloud-storage python-dotenv
```

This brings in AWS and GCS SDKs plus dotenv for managing credentials.

Setting up Credentials

We then create a **.env** file (never commit this) with entries for both providers:

```
AWS_ACCESS_KEY_ID=YOUR_AWS_KEY
AWS_SECRET_ACCESS_KEY=YOUR_AWS_SECRET
GCP_SERVICE_ACCOUNT_JSON=/path/to/service-account.json
GCS_BUCKET_NAME=your-gcs-bucket
S3_BUCKET_NAME=your-s3-bucket
```

Writing Cloud-Upload Script

We then open **cloud_storage.py** and begin with imports and credential loading:

```
import os
from dotenv import load_dotenv
load_dotenv()
# AWS
import boto3
s3 = boto3.client(
    "s3",
    aws_access_key_id=os.getenv("AWS_ACCESS_KEY_ID"),
    aws_secret_access_key=os.getenv("AWS_SECRET_ACCESS_KEY")
)
# GCS
from google.cloud import storage
os.environ["GOOGLE_APPLICATION_CREDENTIALS"] =
os.getenv("GCP_SERVICE_ACCOUNT_JSON")
```

```
gcs_client = storage.Client()
gcs_bucket = gcs_client.bucket(os.getenv("GCS_BUCKET_NAME"))
```

Uploading to S3 and GCS

Next, we define a function that pushes a local file to both buckets:

```
def upload_to_cloud(local_path, s3_key=None,
gcs_blob_name=None):
    s3_key = s3_key or os.path.basename(local_path)
    gcs_blob_name = gcs_blob_name or
os.path.basename(local_path)
    # S3 upload
    s3.upload_file(local_path, os.getenv("S3_BUCKET_NAME"),
s3_key)
    print(f"Uploaded to
S3://{os.getenv('S3_BUCKET_NAME')}/{s3_key}")
    # GCS upload
    blob = gcs_bucket.blob(gcs_blob_name)
    blob.upload_from_filename(local_path)
    print(f"Uploaded to
GCS://{os.getenv('GCS_BUCKET_NAME')}/{gcs_blob_name}")
```

Downloading from S3 and GCS

We then add a function that retrieves files back to local disk:

```
def download_from_cloud(cloud_key, local_path=None,
provider="s3"):
    local_path = local_path or cloud_key
    if provider == "s3":
        s3.download_file(
            os.getenv("S3_BUCKET_NAME"), cloud_key, local_path
        )
```

```
        print(f"Downloaded
S3://{os.getenv('S3_BUCKET_NAME')}/{cloud_key} to
{local_path}")
    elif provider == "gcs":
        blob = gcs_bucket.blob(cloud_key)
        blob.download_to_filename(local_path)
        print(f"Downloaded
GCS://{os.getenv('GCS_BUCKET_NAME')}/{cloud_key} to
{local_path}")
    else:
        raise ValueError("Provider must be 's3' or 'gcs'")
```

Demonstrating Workflow

At the bottom of **cloud_storage.py**, we add a quick demo:

```
if __name__ == "__main__":
    # Assume latest_vaccinations.csv exists locally
    local_file = "latest_vaccinations.csv"
    upload_to_cloud(local_file)
    # Later or elsewhere, download back
    download_from_cloud(local_file, provider="s3")
    download_from_cloud(local_file, provider="gcs")
python cloud_storage.py
```

After running the above script, we can see confirmation messages for each upload and download, ensuring that your vaccination data moves seamlessly between local and cloud storage.

With this setup, we can integrate S3 or GCS into your data pipelines, offloading large files to the cloud and fetching them on demand—all under programmatic control and without manual steps.

Stream-Batch Merging

We get live vaccination events from a Kafka stream, and we also save a historical CSV snapshot. It's tricky to combine raw streams and flat files into one DataFrame because they live in different formats and time windows. We need a process that can take incoming messages, convert them into a pandas table, load the latest batch of CSV files, merge them without duplicates, and keep them in the right chronological order for downstream analytics.

Installing kafka-python

So here, we first create **stream_batch_merge.py** and install the Kafka client.

```
vim stream_batch_merge.py
pip install kafka-python
```

Writing Stream-Batch Merge Script

We first begin with imports and configuration as we did in all the other recipes:

```
import json
import pandas as pd
from kafka import KafkaConsumer
```

We then define settings for your Kafka topic and batch file:

```
KAFKA_TOPIC = "vaccination_events"
BATCH_FILE  = "historical_vaccinations.csv"
BOOTSTRAP_SERVERS = ["localhost:9092"]
```

Consuming Fixed Window of Messages

We then write a function to collect, say, 5 seconds of messages:

```
def consume_stream(timeout=5):
    consumer = KafkaConsumer(
        KAFKA_TOPIC,
        bootstrap_servers=BOOTSTRAP_SERVERS,
        auto_offset_reset="latest",
        value_deserializer=lambda m: json.loads(m.decode("utf-
8"))
    )
    records = []
```

```
    end_time = pd.Timestamp.now().timestamp() + timeout
    print("Consuming stream for", timeout, "seconds…")
    for message in consumer:
        records.append(message.value)
        if pd.Timestamp.now().timestamp() >= end_time:
            break
    consumer.close()
    return records
```

Converting Stream to DataFrame

After this, we then parse the collected JSON into a DataFrame:

```
def stream_to_df(records):
    df_stream = pd.json_normalize(records)
    # Ensure same columns as batch
    df_stream = df_stream[["location", "date",
"daily_vaccinations"]]
    df_stream["date"] = pd.to_datetime(df_stream["date"])
    return df_stream
```

Merging with Historical Batch

There is a function that loads the CSV snapshot and merges:

```
def merge_with_batch(df_stream):
    df_batch = pd.read_csv(BATCH_FILE, parse_dates=["date"])

    # Combine and drop duplicates on location+date
    combined = pd.concat([df_batch, df_stream],
ignore_index=True)
    combined.drop_duplicates(subset=["location", "date"],
keep="last", inplace=True)
```

```
    # Sort for chronological integrity
    combined.sort_values(["location", "date"], inplace=True)
    combined.reset_index(drop=True, inplace=True)

    # Overwrite the batch file for next cycle
    combined.to_csv(BATCH_FILE, index=False)

    print("Merged", len(df_stream), "stream records; batch now
has", combined.shape[0], "rows")
    return combined
```

At the bottom of **stream_batch_merge.py**, we then orchestrate all the steps:

```
if __name__ == "__main__":
    # 1. Consume new events
    records = consume_stream(timeout=5)

    if not records:
        print("No new events received.")
    else:
        # 2. Convert to DataFrame
        df_stream = stream_to_df(records)
        print(df_stream.head())
        # 3. Merge with batch CSV
        merged_df = merge_with_batch(df_stream)
        print(merged_df.tail(5))
python stream_batch_merge.py
```

After running the above script, we can observe printed messages showing how many events arrived, a preview of the new rows, and final batch size. The tail of **merged_df** confirms that new stream rows appear correctly interleaved with historical records.

This whole setup automates the alignment of real-time streams and batch snapshots. Each run consumes fresh events, merges them into the CSV, drops duplicates, sorts chronologically, and writes back a unified store for analysis—no manual stitching required.

Retry and Backoff Logic

Now although the script fetches data from a vaccination API, but occasional rate limits or network hiccups cause **requests.get** to fail with 429 or 500 errors. A single retry often succeeds, yet without a backoff you risk hammering the server. We need to wrap our HTTP calls so that failures trigger a series of spaced retries, backing off exponentially to respect API limits and recover gracefully from transient faults.

Installing 'tenacity'

We first install tenacity alongside requests:

```
pip install tenacity requests
```

That brings in both libraries.

Writing Retry Decorator

Then we open **retry_backoff.py**, import the tools and define a fetch function with decorators:

```
import requests
from tenacity import (
    retry,
    stop_after_attempt,
    wait_exponential,
    retry_if_exception_type
)
API_URL = "https://api.somedomain.com/vaccinations"
@retry(

retry=retry_if_exception_type((requests.exceptions.RequestExce
ption,)),
    stop=stop_after_attempt(5),
    wait=wait_exponential(multiplier=1, min=2, max=30),
```

```
    reraise=True
)
def fetch_with_retry(params=None, headers=None):
    """Fetch JSON from API with retries and exponential
backoff."""
    response = requests.get(API_URL, params=params,
headers=headers, timeout=10)
    response.raise_for_status()
    return response.json()
```

In the aboer, each parameter does the following:

- **`retry_if_exception_type`** retries on network and HTTP exceptions.
- **`stop_after_attempt(5)`** gives up after five tries.
- **`wait_exponential`** starts with 2 s, doubling each time, capped at 30 s.
- **`reraise=True`** surfaces the final error if all attempts fail.

Using Retry Function

At the bottom of **`retry_backoff.py`**, we can then add an execution block:

```
if __name__ == "__main__":
    try:
        data = fetch_with_retry(params={"date": "2021-10-01"})
        print("Fetched records:", len(data.get("records",
[])))
    except Exception as e:
        print("Failed to fetch after retries:", e)
```

After running the **`python retry_backoff.py`**, it shows automatic retries with spaced delays whenever a transient failure occurs.

Custom Backoff Without tenacity

If you prefer a minimal dependency, then try to implement your own loop:

```
import time
```

```
def fetch_with_backoff(params=None, max_attempts=5):
    delay = 2
    for attempt in range(1, max_attempts + 1):
        try:
            resp = requests.get(API_URL, params=params,
timeout=10)
            resp.raise_for_status()
            return resp.json()
        except requests.exceptions.RequestException as err:
            print(f"Attempt {attempt} failed: {err}")
            if attempt == max_attempts:
                raise
            time.sleep(delay)
            delay = min(delay * 2, 30)
```

You can call it the same way:

```
if __name__ == "__main__":
    try:
        data = fetch_with_backoff(params={"date": "2021-10-
01"})
        print("Fetched records:", len(data.get("records",
[])))
    except Exception as e:
        print("Final failure:", e)
```

By wrapping your HTTP calls in retry-and-backoff logic—either with tenacity or a custom loop—you protect your pipeline from transient API failures and rate limits, ensuring robust, respectful data retrieval.

GraphQL and REST Hybrid

We might need info like vaccine details by country and date, which you can get from a GraphQL API, while your main vaccination counts come from a REST CSV. It's a pain to query GraphQL manually and reshape its nested JSON into pandas, and merging with REST data just adds more complexity. We've got to write code that sends a GraphQL POST request, normalizes its response into a flat table, then merges those results with our CSV-derived DataFrame so that every daily record carries both count and metadata.

So here, we first open the **graphql_rest_hybrid.py** together, and bring in the requests and pandas too:

```
vim graphql_rest_hybrid.py
import requests
import pandas as pd
```

We then define both the endpoints:

```
CSV_URL = (
    "https://github.com/owid/covid-19-data/"
    "raw/master/public/data/vaccinations/vaccinations.csv"
)
GRAPHQL_URL = "https://api.example.com/graphql"
```

Writing GraphQL Query

Next, we then create a string with our query, requesting manufacturer and date per country:

```
query = """
query($start: String!, $end: String!) {
  vaccineRecords(filter: {date_between: {start: $start, end:
$end}}) {
    country
    date
    manufacturer
  }
}
"""
variables = {
    "start": "2021-01-01",
```

```
    "end":   "2021-12-31"
}
```

Fetching and Normalizing GraphQL Data

We then send a POST request and check for errors:

```
resp = requests.post(
    GRAPHQL_URL,
    json={"query": query, "variables": variables},
    headers={"Content-Type": "application/json"}
)
resp.raise_for_status()
data = resp.json()["data"]["vaccineRecords"]
```

Next, we do a call to **`pd.json_normalize`** flattens the list of records into a DataFrame:

```
gdf = pd.json_normalize(data)
gdf["date"] = pd.to_datetime(gdf["date"])
print(gdf.head())
```

Loading REST-Based Vaccination Counts

Post this, we pull our main CSV with REST:

```
rdf = pd.read_csv(
    CSV_URL,
    usecols=["location", "date", "daily_vaccinations"],
    parse_dates=["date"]
)
```

Merging GraphQL and REST Data

Now here, let us assume the **`country`** in GraphQL matches **`location`** in our CSV, so here we merge on those keys:

```
combined = pd.merge(
    rdf,
    gdf.rename(columns={"country": "location"}),
    on=["location", "date"],
    how="left"
)
```

Now here, there is a quick info check which confirms that counts and manufacturer metadata co-exist:

```
print(combined.info())
print(combined.head())
```

Verifying Hybrid Table

We can also now look for rows where manufacturer is missing—indicating no GraphQL record for that date:

```
missing_meta = combined["manufacturer"].isna().sum()
print(f"Rows without manufacturer info: {missing_meta}")
```

After this, we inspect a few of those to ensure logic is correct, then save the enriched table:

```
combined.to_csv("vaccinations_with_manufacturer.csv",
index=False)
print("Saved hybrid data with manufacturer metadata")
```

With this approach, we seamlessly query a GraphQL endpoint, flatten its nested JSON into a pandas table, and merge it with REST-based CSV data. Our final DataFrame carries both daily vaccination counts and metadata from both sources, ready for unified analysis.

Summary

We have come to the end of this chapter, and of our book. We learned how to schedule daily API pulls to automatically fetch the latest vaccination CSV, ensuring that our data would stay current without manual intervention. Using PyMongo, we connected to MongoDB, retrieved document-based metadata, and seamlessly merged it with our CSV records in Pandas. We integrated cloud storage by uploading and downloading large files via Boto3 for S3 and Google Cloud Storage for

GCS, embedding those operations directly into our workflows.

We worked with a lot of data by using Kafka to get information about vaccinations, changing it into DataFrames, adding it to old CSV files, and making sure the order was the same. To protect our API calls against rate limits and transient failures, we wrapped requests in retry-and-backoff logic using Tenacity and demonstrated a custom implementation. Finally, we queried a GraphQL endpoint, flattened its nested JSON into a Pandas table using the **`json_normalize`** function, and merged those results with our REST-sourced vaccination counts. Each recipe demonstrated how to automate and combine various data sources, including REST, JSON, NoSQL, cloud storage, streaming, and GraphQL, into unified, analysis-ready DataFrames.

Index

Thank You

www.ingramcontent.com/pod-product-compliance
Lightning Source LLC
Chambersburg PA
CBHW080216170726
48282CB00030B/1137
9789349174993